Arthur Marwick
WOMEN AT WAR

1914–1918

FONTANA PAPERBACKS
in association with
The Imperial War Museum

First published by Fontana Paperbacks 1977
Copyright © Trustees of Imperial War Museum and
Professor Arthur Marwick 1977
Copyright © Original Text Professor Arthur Marwick 1977

Designed by Trevor Vincent
Phototypeset by Tradespools Ltd, Frome, Somerset
Made and printed in Great Britain by
William Collins Sons & Co. Ltd, Glasgow

Contents

Preface

The First World War was the first total war in history, a colossal and horrific experience for all who lived through it. Already, before 1914 was out, it was being referred to as 'the Great War'. It was a measure of the British Government's recognition of the significance of this great watershed in history that, in 1917, it established the Imperial War Museum (originally to be called the National War Museum) to commemorate the heroic endeavours of all who had served in whatever capacity. Since the contributions which women were making to the national effort were being widely praised, it was only natural that a Women's War Work Sub-Committee of the Imperial War Museum should also be established, with Lady Norman as chairman and Miss Agnes Conway as Secretary ('chairman', of course, was the word used by Lady Norman, and the other women of the time).

Throughout the later stages of the war Lady Norman and Miss Agnes Conway contacted every individual and every association which had any conceivable association with women's war work. They were thus able to assemble a unique contemporary collection of documentary and photographic material. This collection fills over 200 box-files in the Imperial War Museum Library, and forms the first major archive source on which this book is based. In addition the Museum has a number of separate collections of private papers belonging to women of the period.

Among the Government departments contacted by Lady Norman and Miss Conway was, naturally enough, the Ministry of Reconstruction, a Ministry set up towards the end of the war to deal with problems of post-war planning, including the question of the role of women after the war. However, as can be seen from the Ministry records, the civil servants there did not welcome Miss Conway's inquiries, and one of them minuted grudgingly: 'It is, I suppose, difficult to refuse to give them such papers eventually, though I fail to see what value they would have for the Museum.' Every historian of the modern period will recognize this archetypal civil service attitude towards historical research. But, of course, the many different departmental records relating to all those aspects of the war in which women were involved are now open for study: these records form the second major source for this book, together with the Cabinet and associated records housed in a separate section of the Public Record Office.

The major part of the records pertaining to the moderate suffragist organizations, in particular Mrs Fawcett's National Union of Women's Suffrage Societies, is to be found in the Fawcett Library, London, while some other important papers are preserved in the Archive Department of the Manchester Public Library. The main collection of suffragette papers is in the Museum of London; and the Sylvia Pankhurst papers are at the International Institute for Social History in Amsterdam; there are also relevant papers in the National Library of Scotland, Edinburgh.

Together these form the third major set of archive sources for this work.

In preparation for the Imperial War Museum Exhibition which accompanies the publication of this book, reminiscences were invited from women who had lived through the First World War. Obviously, memories which go back sixty years must be approached with some caution; nonetheless, personal reminiscences of this sort, when balanced against the other types of evidence, provide a valuable additional dimension. The reminiscences of the major figures have, naturally, long since appeared in print.

Finally, this book draws upon the immense range of other published sources, Government Reports, Census data, newspapers, novels, and polemical tracts of one sort or another, of which I made considerable use in my book *The Deluge: British Society and the First World War*, which was first published in 1965.

Surprisingly, very little has in fact been written on women's experience during the war. There have been many books on the suffragist and suffragette movements, such as Roger Fulford's *Votes for Women* (1957), Constance Rover's *Woman's Suffrage and Party Politics in Britain* (1967), Andrew Rosen's *Rise Up Women!* (1974), and Antonia Raeburn's *The Militant Suffragettes* (1973), but all of these bring their main story to a close in 1914, with, at most, a cursory glance at the war. David Mitchell's *Women on the Warpath* (1966) contains much interesting information, but is essentially a series of biographical studies, rather than an analysis of woman's war experience as a whole.

David Morgan, in his brief *Suffragists and Liberals* (1975), gives due prominence to the war, but is concerned only with the exclusive world of high politics. In an article 'Politicians and the Woman's Vote 1914–1918' in the historical journal *History* (1974), which is also, as the title indicates, concerned with politics, Martin Pugh, with all that love of the brilliant paradox which characterizes the learned article, actually argues that the war hindered women's progress towards the franchise, resulting in their accepting less in 1918 than they would have done had there been no war. As will become clear in the course of this book, I believe this to be an absurd contention.

Historians too often prefer to focus the spotlight exclusively on the leading actors. This is fair enough for the years before 1914 which were dominated by a handful of powerful figures among the suffragists and the suffragettes, and by the reactions of major politicians such as Balfour, Asquith, and Lloyd George. But during the war the stage becomes crowded. Now it is the actions of ordinary unknown women which begin also to affect the destinies of all women. In this book I have tried to bring out something of what it was like to be an ordinary woman living through the First World War.

But is that an appropriate task for a mere male? That must be left for each reader to decide for herself, or himself. But preferably only after reading the book. Meantime I would just like to comment that in reading Ruth Adam's excellent, if all too brief, *A Woman's Place, 1910–1975* (1975), I was at least as much struck by the illumination this book casts on the role of men as it does on the role of women.

For serious students and scholars who want to follow up these fascinating topics and develop them for themselves I have included a very bare list of references.

Acknowledgements

I should like to thank Dr Alice Prochaska of the Public Record Office who, by putting at my disposal her enormous expertise in the departmental records relating to women, saved me many days of painful searching. Mrs Victoria Moger of the Library of the Museum of London, Miss Kathleen Waller of the Fawcett Library, Mrs Jean Ayton of the Archives Department, Manchester Public Library, Mr S. M. Simpson of the National Library of Scotland, and Ms M. W. H. Schreuder of the International Institute of Social History, Amsterdam, also greatly facilitated my work. I am indebted to my colleague, Bernard Waites, who not only read the proofs, but shared with me his own perceptions of British society in the First World War.

The invitation to do this book came in the first place from Dr Christopher Dowling of the Imperial War Museum; I am most grateful to him, and, in particular, to Jean Liddiard who did much of the work in regard to the detailed picture research and the collection of personal reminiscences, and to their colleagues in the Department of Education and Publications, the Library, and the Department of Documents.

My best thanks to Peggy Mackay and Terry Brady who typed the first draft of this book, and my renewed thanks to Peggy Mackay who prepared the final version for publication.

With the publishers and the Imperial War Museum, I am most grateful to those individuals who have given me permission to make use of copyright material in the text, especially all those whose personal reminiscences are deposited in the Imperial War Museum's archives, and those correspondents who have supplied information to the organizers of the 'Women at War' exhibition. While every effort has been made to trace copyright holders, in a few cases this has not proved possible and the publishers would be grateful to hear from any such not duly acknowledged.

All the illustrations in the text are from the collection at the Imperial War Museum, with the exception of those on the following pages: 10, 17, 26: *Illustrated London News*, 1914; 14–15: *Daily Mail* Library, catalogue of 'The Sweated Industries Exhibition' 1906; 19: The School Council, Royal Free Hospital School of Medicine; 23 (top left and bottom): The Trustees of the National Library of Scotland; 23 (top right), 24, 25: The Trustees of the Fawcett Library; 32, 33, 52–3, 152, 159 (bottom): The Museum of London; 133: Mrs Doris Macdonald; 134 (top): Mrs K. Mosley. With the Imperial War Museum and the publishers, I am most grateful to these institutions and individuals for permission to reproduce their photographs.

The cut-out figures of women at work, which appear on this page and elsewhere in the early and latter parts of the book, date from 1917. Originally they were possibly sold for charity and this set was collected just after the First World War as part of the children's section of the Imperial War Museum.

Let the Pianola Piano bring you happiness in 1914.

Do not merely hope for increased happiness in the year that is before you ensure it by purchasing a Pianola Piano. There is no other investment you can make which will so surely bring pleasure to you and every member of your household, for by its means everyone can play the music they love. Day in, day out, through many a year, the influence of the world's sweetest music will brighten and cheer you through the dull routine of life.

The Pianola Piano is the genuine Pianola combined with the STEINWAY, WEBER, STECK, or STROUD Piano. You are invited to play at Æolian Hall, or to write for Illustrated Catalogue "H."

THE ORCHESTRELLE COMPANY, ÆOLIAN HALL,
135-6-7, New Bond Street, LONDON, W.

CHAPTER ONE

MEN, WOMEN AND WAR

Women in Society

The actual role and status of women in any society is largely determined by the particular conventions, preconceptions, and prejudices existing about the nature and position of women. Because of its very intensity as an experience, because of the way it projected people into new situations, the First World War revealed very starkly the assumptions and attitudes which were widely held about women, and the sorts of discrimination which were customarily practised against them. Some attitudes may emerge as practically identical with those still current today; others will be seen as belonging specifically to the context of the Edwardian era.

But perhaps there are some eternal, innate disadvantages from which women suffer, some to be diminished by the more or less neutral forces of advancing technology, others possibly only to be dealt with by 'positive' discrimination. Broadly speaking, and ignoring the exceptions, it may be said that women tend to suffer from three main biological handicaps: lesser muscular power than men; the time and energy devoted to child-bearing and childrearing; and menstruation. Perhaps one should also add the fact of differential ageing: girls usually mature more quickly than boys but women in early middle age tend to show their years more obviously than men: women take the last trick in old age, but the aged of both sexes got short shrift from Edwardian society. No doubt, there are special handicaps from which men suffer; and no doubt there are special advantages possessed by women (infant mortality was higher among males; but this worked out to the severe disadvantage of surviving females). But in the era with which we are concerned, when women for the first time were beginning to take on new tasks, it was with the disadvantages of women that society concerned itself.

Technological change has diminished, perhaps even removed, the significance of, say, women's lesser physical strength. But it must be remembered that many of the technological developments which we take for granted today had not yet appeared at the time of the First World War. Doubtless women (and men) today are little better off for the advent of fish fingers, deep freezes and deodorants. It is, however, particularly crucial to the experience of women in 1914 that there was no DDT, no detergents, no tampons, and no oral contraceptives. Men wore their hair short in the Edwardian and First World War period: lice were a problem for everyone, but perhaps most of all for the young woman cultivating her tresses as 'woman's crowning glory'. It is continually stressed that women travelling around on war work need to take with them everywhere a fine comb. Women, whether as housewives, housemaids, or scrubbers (the word was then still used in its literal meaning without the male chauvinist overtones of today) were in the front line of the war against dirt. As we follow women's new pilgrimage across the country and

Advertisement for Pianola in
Illustrated London News,
17 January 1914

11

overseas in their part in waging war against Germany, we encounter from time to time the advice that they should take with them disposable, rather than washable, sanitary towels.

Wherever women were travelling, or wherever they were being congregated together in groups, there was always among the authorities, women as well as men, a great preoccupation with the topic of 'morality'. We shall find, too, and this is maybe something which hasn't really changed much, that wherever there are groups of younger women brought together, particularly in new circumstances, there will always be groups of men to spread rumours, often totally ill-founded, about their immorality.

Yet if the war starkly revealed Edwardian assumptions about women, and perhaps also certain unchanging assumptions, it also offered unique possibilities for bringing about changes in their position and status. The major historical questions are: Were the new opportunities offered by the war permanent, and were the areas of discrimination against women reduced? Did the war enhance the status of women in society? Did it mark a definite step forward towards equal rights, or did it (as Martin Pugh has argued in regard to women's suffrage) actually harm their cause rather than improve it?

These questions, in turn, bring up the problem of the role and significance of the militant suffragettes. If it really was the war that brought votes for women, was suffragette violence then irrelevant, or perhaps even harmful to the women's cause? Does not the way in which many of the most militant suffragette leaders took up an extremely militaristic, and even bloodthirsty stance during the war suggest that it was possibly something odd in their psychology which led them into the militant suffragette campaign in the first place?

These are merely questions. What one can do is to demonstrate the chronological stages through which women's role developed and expanded. After all, the Great War lasted for over four years, uncoiling with the loathesome slowness of a vast and hideous boa-constrictor. The many developments affecting women did not all happen at once. The first phase of the war, the period of 'War Emergency' followed by that of 'Business as Usual', lasted from August 1914 to the early summer of 1915: apart from the voluntary activities undertaken and organized by a minority of upper-class women, there were no really striking changes as far as the broad mass of British women were concerned. There followed the first of the two major turning-points in the history of women during the war: the new Coalition Government, established in May 1915, set up a separate Ministry of Munitions which positively and directly encouraged the enrolment of women in munitions factories. The still more important, and indeed absolutely crucial, turning-point came with the introduction of universal military conscription for men in May 1916, following upon the unsatisfactory Conscription Act of January 1916 which was confined to unmarried men. The enforced withdrawal of men from the domestic front provided the critical impetus towards full scale employment of women in all types of occupations. The final eighteen months of the war are characterized by a still more efficient organization of the war effort by the Lloyd George Coalition Government established in December 1916: it was in this period that the Women's Auxiliary Military Services were set up; this was also a time of increasing war weariness and considerable hardship for the ordinary housewife.

The absolutely central phenomenon in the changing position of women was their movement into new jobs. Essentially, this happened in three ays: through the private initiative of voluntary organizations; through rect government action; and through the working out of the forces of he market. To begin with, relatively small numbers of women were recruited through voluntary patriotic organizations set up by upper-class ladies into such activities as volunteer policework, driving officers round, or helping out in canteens or on farms. Then, in 1915, the Government, very tentatively at first, and then more positively after the setting up of the Ministry of Munitions, began deliberately to stimulate the recruitment of women into the munitions factories and then into many other occupations. Some of the voluntary patriotic organizations continued throughout the war, but many of them became absorbed in the Government's own efforts to enlist the services of women. Market forces operated only in a small way in the early days. If a husband went off to the war, leaving, say, a small one-man business, his wife would often simply take over his responsibilities. Later on, as more and more vacancies developed in all sorts of occupations (and here, conscription for men was crucial), women were tempted in by new opportunities and higher wages. Of course, although the principles of private enterprise still predominated in 1914, British society, particularly in war, was very far from being based on a pure market economy. The British trade union movement was already strong enough to ensure that women could not in all cases simply walk into men's jobs, especially if there was no guarantee that in so doing they would not depress wage standards; and since the early nineteenth century, the Government, through various factory acts, had taken special interest in the conditions under which women laboured. So, as women moved into new jobs, there were all kinds of reactions and implications in regard to trade union responses, Government action, and, indeed, in the setting up of new organizations among women themselves. The fact is, you cannot study the history of women without at the same time studying the history of men.

British Women in August 1914

Grinding, back-breaking work had been the lot of most women for centuries. It had been for men too; but, on the whole, where women worked, it was under conditions even more unpleasant. In the underdeveloped countries of today women still often do the most arduous work in the fields. In Britain, save for some parts of Scotland, the woman labourer on the land had long since disappeared by 1914, though life for the wife or daughter of the farmworker or small farmer was certainly long and taxing enough. In the Edwardian period British women still did surface work at the coal tips, dirty, unskilled, manual labour. For over a century women had been a central source of labour for the Lancashire cotton mills; single girls predominated, but married women were also employed.

In general, the respectable British working man preferred his wife not to work outside the home. The skilled coal-face worker was the highest paid 'aristocrat' of British labour in 1914; for his wife the income brought in by himself and his miner sons was enough to maintain the household at a reasonably adequate level, but life still meant too many pregnancies, a constant battle against coal dust with only the most rudimentary washing facilities, and a constant and high risk of losing one or more bread-winners in a pit disaster. At the lower end, women of the working classes were sucked into an abyss of squalor and filth where female sluttishness was a norm; at the highest level, they had to keep up an image of working-class respectability, scouring doorsteps and keeping

TOP LEFT Women as industrial drudges: A Bromsgrove Nail-Maker, *c.* 1906
Sweated Trades:
FAR LEFT (1) Match-Box Makers, *c.* 1906
ABOVE (2) Sack-Making, *c.* 1906
LEFT (3) Cardboard-box Making, *c.* 1906

15

clothes clean, in a physical environment which lent little aid to su
aspirations.

The unskilled industrial work undertaken by women paid very badly.
Still worse were the various 'domestic' and 'sweated' trades: dressmaking,
millinery, artificial flowermaking, boxmaking, and so on. These trades
were carried on either in a woman's own home, or in some tiny crowded
workshop, beyond the reach of the overworked factory inspectorate;
usually on piecework, the women were paid derisory sums for producing
quantities of goods which required inhumanly long hours of work. In
many areas the most usual 'career' for girls was that of domestic service.
Just how much this humiliating, exacting, underpaid job was detested
was to be shown once the war had opened some alternatives. Just a cut
above this was to work as a shop assistant; often, however, almost as
humiliating and not much more rewarding. Clerical work for women
greatly expanded in the Edwardian period, but always the salaries were
lower than those of the male clerks they replaced. Florence Nightingale
had changed nursing from the resort of the Mrs Gamps of the world to a
respectable profession; but again, the nurses could expect to be kicked
around and badly paid. Educational opportunities had increased greatly
towards the end of the nineteenth century, but often this led to no more
than a teaching post in one of the elementary schools, posts which in
income and status were little, if anything, above that of the governess of
an earlier era.

Before the war, the average wage of women in industrial work was
11s 7d (under 60p) per week, only a third of the average male industrial
wage. A lady factory inspector, not given either to prurience or excita-
bility, reported to a private Committee of Inquiry during the war that in
pre-war days low wages frequently drove waitresses and shop assistants
to occasional prostitution.[1] The link between economic, social and sexual
dependence is upsettingly brought out in a personal experience of
Christopher Addison, a general practitioner who subsequently became
the close political associate of Lloyd George: after, as part of his early
medical training, delivering a baby for a woman in an East End slum, the
woman remarked that for obvious reasons, she could not herself 'oblige'
the young doctor, but that her sister would be delighted to do so.

For the respectable working-class family, it was a sign of status that
the wife did not have to go out to work, but that she kept a tidy house and
turned out decently dressed children. In 1914 the school attendance laws
were thoroughly soggy, susceptible to pressure from employers who
wanted cheap child labour, parents who wanted additional income from
their children, and parents and children who saw little value in schooling.
Officially the school-leaving age was fourteen, but children who had
secured a certificate of 'proficiency' or of regular attendance could leave
at thirteen. Local authorities might if they liked (not many did) forbid
all work by children under the age of fourteen. In some industrial areas,
including Lancashire, the 'half-timer' was common: girls and boys of
twelve or over who worked up to 33 hours a week in the factories and
went to school the rest of the time. Children, if able enough, could transfer
at eleven or twelve to a secondary school, and thus spend their last few
years there. But most working-class children, even if they stayed on
full-time to fourteen, simply endured a repetitive elementary education.
In the areas where it was common, the trade unions favoured the institution of the 'half-timer'. But for the aspiring working-class family it was
again usually an indication of status to keep girls as well as boys at
school until at least the leaving age had been reached. It was generally

Advertisement for
Elliman's embrocation in
Illustrated London News,
25 April 1914

16

THE GIRL OF TO-DAY

Has that same sound faith "Faith in Elliman's"; the remarks upon facing page also apply to this picture.

ELLIMAN, SONS & CO. Embrocation Manufacturers. SLOUGH, ENGLAND.

LEFT Women students from
Bedford College University of
London engaged in botanical
work in 1914. Ladies'
Supplement III *Illustrated
London News*, 14 March 1914

RIGHT Medical graduates
c. 1894–6 from the Royal Free
Hospital School of Medicine,
founded in 1874 as the London
School for Women
Top Row left to right:
Miss Thorne, Miss Weir,
Miss Caine, Miss Fitter,
Miss Le Pelley, Mrs Wilks,
Miss Meakin, Miss B. Webb,
Miss Billet, Miss Vernon,
Miss Jacobi
Second Row left to right:
Mrs Marshall, Miss Bentham,
Miss Boyle, Miss Jones,
Miss Appel, Mrs Berry,
Miss Knowles, Miss Sharman,
Miss M. Sturge, Miss Maitland,
Miss Shepperd, Miss Chad-
burn, Mrs Hemming,
Miss Swatman, Miss Despard,
Miss Turner, Miss Crosfield,
Miss Handson
Third Row left to right:
Miss H. Russell (standing),
Miss Cargill, Mrs Keith,
Mrs Boyd, Mrs Scharlieb,
Mrs Garrett-Anderson,
Miss Cook, Miss Walker,
Miss Ellaby, Miss H. Webb,
Miss Macdonald, Miss Bond
Front Row left to right:
Miss Douie,
Miss J. B. Henderson,
Miss Leney, Miss Aldrich-
Blake, Miss Boyle,
Miss Williams,
Miss Cruikshank,
Miss H. Armitage,
Miss Sutherland, Miss Flint

thought much less worthwhile to keep girls on at school than it might be for their brothers, so the girls would be seen off into one of the respectable but badly paid jobs already described, such as shop assistant or secretary.

For middle- and upper-class families, status was most usually achieved by ensuring that both mother and daughters did as little arduous and useful work as possible. The better off the family, the more servants there were to preserve the wife from the duties of housekeeping; if the daughters were to be educated, it was to make them graciously decorative, but suitably discreet, foils to their future husbands.

Some of the charities and other voluntary activities which middle- and upper-class women undertook to fill out their leisure hours were in fact in themselves eminently worthwhile, and could involve the development of considerable organizational skills on the part of the women concerned. Some women too, sometimes with the encouragement of men, were insisting on making the most of the educational opportunities which had opened up from the late nineteenth century onwards. Women could take degrees at the Scottish and at the English provincial universities: there were women's colleges at Oxford and Cambridge, respectfully sited on the outskirts of these ancient towns, though women could not actually take degrees at either university. A few women were penetrating into the higher professions: there were women doctors, and women university teachers. Almost without exception these women were unmarried. Expansion in the social services created some opportunities for women in the Civil Service. The lady factory inspectors formed a tiny but influential group, who were to prove of great importance as the new war situation developed.

Outwardly, Edwardian society still observed strictly most of the moral canons of Victorianism. In the highest social circles, centring on Edward VII himself, there was undoubtedly much permissiveness, but it was not a permissiveness that could ever be publicly boasted of, so that the risks for an Edwardian lady were always considerably higher, and the freedoms considerably lower, than for an Edwardian gentleman. Middle-class,

RIGHT Women students from
the Royal Free Hospital
School of Medicine in the
Physiology Laboratory,
c. 1899

and respectable working-class society, aspired, without much hypocrisy, to a genuine observance of Victorian standards; but behaviour which could be condoned, or not known about in a man, could spell ruin for a woman. Most feminists in the Edwardian period believed in what they called 'purity'; their aim was to get all men to observe the ideal standard which respectable women had to observe. In the 1880s, Mrs Josephine Butler had led a successful campaign against the existence of licensed brothels in garrison towns. Venereal diseases, though not much mentioned in public, form an ominous shadow lurking on the consciousness of Edwardian society. To moralists they were, together with illegitimate parenthood, 'the wages of sin'. Feminists were more preoccupied with the way in which men who had resorted to prostitutes communicated the disease to their innocent wives, and children. They were resolutely opposed to any idea of medical inspection for prostitutes, as being both demeaning to womanhood, and encouraging what they described as the 'animal instincts' in men. Partly, no doubt, because women can be asymptomatic carriers of syphilis, the theory was widespread that promiscuous women were the originators of the disease. And some men actually believed, or affected to believe, that a cure lay in having sexual intercourse with a young girl.

There were women in the Edwardian period arguing for 'liberation' for women, rather than 'repression' or 'purification' for men. But apart from the taboos and conventions from which it was hard for even the most strong-willed woman to escape, there was the problem of the chanciness of existing methods of contraception. Rubber male and female contraceptives had been developed in the previous century; and there was a whole range of other secret remedies on the market, spermicides, pessaries, and, of course, abortifacients, ranging from the dubious, to the irrelevant, to the downright dangerous. Upper- and middle-class families were practising contraception within the family unit: but the woman who sought to go outside the family was still standing on shifting sands.

After the long Victorian silence in which novels and other literature had come near to denying the existence of any sexual drives at all in women, some Edwardian novels and plays were beginning to hint again that women indeed might have greater sexual appetites than men. Eleanor Glyn's *Three Weeks*, first published in 1907, was a best-seller, though also violently attacked as being sordid and immoral. Eleanor Glyn later said of her heroine that she was 'beyond the ordinary laws of immorality'. 'If I was making a study of a tiger,' she added, 'I would not give it the attributes of a spaniel, because the public, and myself, might prefer a spaniel.' But usually even the most *avant-garde* Edwardian novels carried the implication that celibacy was no real hardship for a woman. One of the finest tributes to liberated but independent womanhood was made by a male author and is to be found in the celebrated play of 1911, *Hindle Wakes*, by the Manchester journalist and playwright Harold Brighouse: after a series of speeches upon which the most ardent young feminist of today could scarcely improve, the factory girl heroine refuses to marry the boss's son who has got her pregnant. Perhaps the most curious phenomenon of all is that when Baden-Powell's new semi-militaristic movement for boys, the Boy Scouts, was followed by the sister organization, the Girl Guides, the advice to the girls was slightly more explicit on the dangers of masturbation than was that given to the boys. *The Hand-book for Girl Guides* (1912) written by Agnes Baden-Powell with her brother's collaboration warned that: 'All secret bad habits are evil and dangerous, lead to hysteria and lunatic asylums, and serious illness is the result ... Evil practices dare not face an honest person; they lead you on to blindness, paralysis and loss of memory.'

One male argument for opposing votes for women was that women did not play a part in the armed defence of their country. In a country where there was no military conscription, as there was in most continental countries, few men really expected to be called upon to bear arms either. Equally there were women who, though miles away in attitude from the militant suffragettes, did seek a close involvement in military activities. Some of the most active supporters of the National Service League, a pressure group in favour of military conscription for men, were women. In the later stages of the Irish crisis before the European war broke out, some Ulster women began arming and drilling in preparation for the impending civil war. A Mrs J. C. Patterson achieved a special distinction in the Edwardian years for the number of youths from poor and broken homes that she encouraged to enlist in the professional army. As the *Tatler* put it shortly after the outbreak of war: 'True women of Britain have from time immemorial done recruiting work in its highest sense; that is to say, in using their influence to incite men to deeds of valour.' The *Tatler*, however, added, 'these women have never endeavoured to take the place of recruiting sergeants'.

The Edwardian period was a time of war scares, and of a widely held belief that a conflict with Germany must come sometime. Actually it was experience in the Sudan which led Sergeant-Major Baker to suggest the formation of bands of mounted nurses who would ride out to the actual scenes of action. The FANY (First Aid Nursing Yeomanry) was founded in 1907, a group of adventurous upper-class ladies who could afford to provide their own mounts. The Women's Convoy Corps was founded in the same year. In 1909 the War Office published a Scheme for Voluntary Aid to the Sick and Wounded, and the Territorial Force County Associations were charged with the responsibility of organizing what were to be called Voluntary Aid Detachments. These Detachments were to consist of both men and women, but in practise, since the main work of the Detachments would be in the sphere of nursing, most of the recruits were women. The actual management of the Detachments was put in the hands of two famous voluntary Societies, The British Red Cross Society, and the St John's Ambulance and Brigade Associations. The VAD Organization came into existence in 1910. One single Woman's Voluntary Aid Detachment normally consisted of 23 women, but in popular usage, the initials VAD came to be used to refer to one individual member. Although the Detachments were organized for home service in case of an invasion, it was not then contemplated that they would serve overseas. However, early in 1914 a list was drawn up of members 'willing and qualified to take service abroad in case of emergency'. There was still no question at this time but that VAD work was voluntary and unpaid. The major professional organizations, mustering just over 3,000 trained military nurses in August 1914, were Queen Alexandra's Imperial Military Nursing Service and the Territorial Force Nursing Services.

In 1914 trade union organization had scarcely touched women workers. The main aim of the protagonists of women's trade unionism, women of middle-class backgrounds like Mary Macarthur and Susan Lawrence, and genuine working-class products like Margaret Bondfield, was the integration of women workers into the old established male trade unions.

Mary Macarthur had played a leading role in organizing the National Union of Women Workers which catered for women where, for the time being, there was no opportunity for joining a men's union. Unlike so many of the women activists of the time, Mary Macarthur always used her maiden name, though she was married to the Labour MP, W. C. Anderson.

The Franchise: Suffragists and Suffragettes

The franchise in 1914 was still governed by the provisions of the third Reform Act of 1884. The main qualification was that of being a male householder, for which it was necessary to prove unbroken occupation of the house in question for twelve months prior to the previous 15 July. In 1914 about seven million men were entitled to vote by virtue of the household occupation qualification. In addition, six other types of qualification (of which the most important were the historic 40 shilling freehold franchise and the lodger franchise) entitled a further million men to vote. All in all, just under 60 per cent of the adult male population had the vote, while no women at all had the vote. Half-a-million richer men had two or more votes; in the election of January 1910, two especially well-qualified brothers had between them cast a total of 35 votes.

The first Women's Suffrage Societies were founded in 1867, in Edinburgh, London and Manchester; a year later, two more were founded in Birmingham and Bristol. The National Union of Women's Suffrage Societies (NUWSS), a federation of sixteen individual societies, all with many branches under their care, was founded in 1898 under the leadership of Mrs Millicent Garrett Fawcett (she herself, and her followers, unselfconsciously used the patriarchal form, Mrs Henry Fawcett). Most (not all) of the early suffragists were educated ladies of the upper and middle classes. They had the support of liberal-minded men from the same social background, but also from the emerging Labour movement. Upper-class women suffragists were primarily concerned to secure votes for women on the same (undemocratic) terms as for men. Working-class male sympathizers were primarily concerned to secure universal adult suffrage; and, if it came to a choice, most of them were more interested in universal male suffrage. In between, there were many positions, which frequently ebbed and shifted as the tactical political situation fluctuated.

Many members of the NUWSS were successful professional women who had achieved much in the way of breaking down barriers of male prejudice in such spheres as medicine and education. In a major local government reform towards the end of the nineteenth century, women householders and wives of householders were given the vote in local elections, and were enabled to serve on local councils, where again many NUWSS members gave good service. However, as far as winning the parliamentary vote was concerned, very little had been achieved by the early years of the new century. Thus in 1903 a new woman's organization devoted to 'Deeds not Words' was founded. The new body, The Women's Social and Political Union (WSPU) was very much under the direction of two passionate, and perhaps rather egocentric, members of the Pankhurst family, Mrs Emmeline Pankhurst and her daughter Christabel, though the leadership also included Annie Kenney, a working-class woman from Lancashire. 'Deeds', to begin with, meant heckling and other disruptive tactics at political meetings, and this active campaign was intensified after 1905 when the Liberals, who could be considered more amenable to pressure than the Conservatives, came into power.

There can be no doubt that women's suffrage now became a first class political issue, and most historians would agree that the activist tactics of the WSPU deserve the credit for this. The NUWSS kept up its more genteel activities. Within the male bastion of Parliament, the feminists did have a number of active supporters, and on several occasions there

MISS CHRISTABEL PANKHURST, LL.B.
NATIONAL WOMEN'S SOCIAL & POLITICAL UNION 4 CLEMENTS. INN W C

STARVATION

WAITING FOR A LIVING WAGE

ABOVE Suffragette postcard
LEFT Picture postcard of
Christabel Pankhurst put out
by WSPU
BELOW Picture postcard of
Mrs Pankhurst, Miss Annie
Kenney and Mrs Pethick
Lawrence put out by WSPU

were favourable majorities for extension of the franchise to women; broadly speaking, women's suffrage had the support of quite a large number of rank-and-file Liberals and of a considerably smaller number of leading Conservatives. But the Liberal Prime Minister from 1908 onwards, Asquith, was himself hostile, so that there was no formal Government support. One suffragist summed up the situation neatly when she said that, from her point of view, the Liberals were any army without generals, the Conservatives generals without an army.

After the two elections of 1910, which drastically reduced the Liberal majority, a stalemate seemed to be reached on the suffrage issue. It was now that the frustration felt by the WSPU boiled over into direct violence, and the word 'suffragette', the title of one of the WSPU newspapers, came into popular usage. At the 1911 Derby Emily Davison was killed on the racecourse. Opponents of the suffragettes said that she had deliberately endangered horse and rider, as well as seeking martyrdom for herself: probably this is the correct interpretation, though film of the incident suggests that she may have been simply grabbing for the bridle of the horse in an effort to make a public demonstration which would do as little physical harm as possible to anyone. The suffragettes chained themselves to railings, kicked and scratched policemen. A small bomb damaged the Coronation Chair in Westminster Abbey, paintings (including the Velasquez 'Venus') were slashed, churches, railway stations and, in Scotland, three castles were damaged or destroyed by fire. There was no loss of life. On the other side, police reactions were often extremely brutal. When suffragettes in prison went on hunger strike, they were forcibly fed, despite the extreme hazard to their health. At least one suffragette died as a direct result of her experiences; Emmeline Pankhurst probably would not have survived had not the war intervened. While it seems reasonable to give the WSPU the credit for making women's suffrage a major issue between 1905 and 1910, there is substance in the argument that the extreme activities after 1910 were counter-productive. However, it is not as simple as that: the suffragettes and the Government got locked into a vicious circle in which the harsh responses of the Government seem more blameworthy than the initial provocations of the suffragettes.

In 1912 came the notorious 'Cat and Mouse Act' which allowed the authorities to release suffragettes when hunger striking was bringing them near to death, then to re-arrest them as soon as freedom had restored them to health. To make out the case against the Asquith regime is not to deny that Emmeline Pankhurst, and more particularly, Christabel, seemed to be becoming more and more divorced from reality, more hysterical and more demanding of total loyalty from their supporters. There is a fascinating ambivalence about the sexily posed photograph of Christabel, expressly taken for a picture postcard (p. 23, top left).

During the period of extreme militancy, the NUWSS continued its patient and impressive propaganda work: its numerical strength expanded steadily, perhaps as part of a reaction against suffragette violence, perhaps because suffragette violence had at least brought further attention to the cause, probably because of a mixture of the two. From a membership of 13,161 members in 70 societies in 1909, the NUWSS rose to a membership of 53,000 distributed over 480 societies in March 1914. Within the WSPU there were protests against both extreme militancy and the dictatorship of the Pankhursts. In 1910 Mrs Despard set up the Women's Freedom League (WFL) which, while still militant in approach, eschewed extreme violence. The second Pankhurst daughter, Sylvia, with the general

BELOW Mrs Fawcett in 1915

support of the third daughter, Adela, reacted to the growing hostility which Emmeline and Christabel were showing towards their former associates in the Labour and trade union movement by founding the East London Women's Suffrage Federation among the working-class women in the slums of London's East End. In February 1914 several of the leading male intellectuals and politicians who had been associated with the WSPU, such as Gerald Gould, H. W. Nevinson, Laurence Housman, and George Lansbury, together with some of the more gifted women, including Louisa Garrett Anderson and Evelyn Sharp, formed the United Suffragists and took with them the other WSPU organ, *Votes for Women*, which even after the outbreak of war continued to be a totally uncomprising supporter of women's suffrage. *Suffragette* remained in the hands of Emmeline and Christabel Pankhurst, though Christabel herself, released under the Cat and Mouse Act in 1912, had taken refuge in France where she remained until after the outbreak of war. The Women's Freedom League had its own newspaper, *The Voter*, and Sylvia Pankhurst launched the *Woman's Dreadnought*. There were a number of other women's organizations spread throughout the country, many of them publishing their own literature. But although the suffragettes were making the headlines in the last years before the war, the most influential paper was probably Mrs Fawcett's *Common Cause*. The suffrage issue came up again in Parliament in 1913, when the Liberal Government was itself anxious to amend other unsatisfactory aspects of the franchise, particularly plural voting which operated very much to the advantage of the Conservatives. However, the attempt to move a woman's suffrage amendment to the main Government Bill was frustrated by the Speaker ruling it out of order. To many women, this again suggested that an exclusively male parliamentary system was inflexibly rigged against any serious consideration of their cause.

The Model Illustrated is Royal Worcester No. 666, Price 16/11

LEFT Advertisement for Peter Robinson's in *Illustrated London News*, 2 May 1914

CHAPTER TWO

THE WAR EMERGENCY

August 1914 to May 1915

First Reactions

Bank Holiday Monday in one of the most glorious summers within living memory fell on 3 August. Although very many poorer families were in no position to go away for the holiday, railway stations and seaside towns were more than usually busy. A few days before, the newspapers had been full of impending civil war in Ireland: now they were full of the war which had already broken out between Germany and Austria on one side, and Serbia, Russia and France on the other. On the Bank Holiday afternoon, Sir Edward Grey, Foreign Secretary in the Liberal Government, explained why Britain might be drawn into the continental conflict. News that German troops were passing across Belgium in their march towards France came through the following day; Asquith announced that his Government had served the Germans with an ultimatum expiring at 11 p.m. (midnight in Berlin) calling upon them to withdraw from Belgium.

Although jingoistic fervour affected vast sections of the British population, many leading intellectuals, liberals and socialists were most unhappy about the turn of events and believed that Britain should stay out of the war. Among them was Mrs Henry Fawcett, leader of the NUWSS who addressed a Women's Protest against the war in the Kingsway Hall on the evening of 4 August. But by the next day much of the opposition to the war had evaporated: now that Britain was in the war, many argued, there was a clear duty to give every support to the national cause, back up the troops, ensure national survival, and bring the war to a successful conclusion as quickly as possible. Mrs Fawcett issued this message: 'Now is the time for resolute effort and self-sacrifice on the part of every one of us to help our country. Let us show ourselves worthy of citizenship, whether our claim to it be recognized or not.' The suffragists in London set up a new Women's Service Bureau to provide information about jobs for those women who were thrown out of work by the war crisis, and suggestions for other women on how they could help the national effort. Mrs Fawcett and the NUWSS steered a skilful and sensitive course, conducting among other things, an agitation against the 'scanty representation of women on Government Relief Committees'.[2] By the end of the year they had set up a Women's Interests Committee, which while partly concerned to make it easier for women to play a useful part in the war effort, and indeed to insist that women could do many jobs just as well as men, was also concerned to make sure that women were not exploited as voluntary or cheap labour.

Contrary to what is often said, Mrs Pankhurst was to begin with much more guarded in giving her support to the national effort. Of course, suffragettes were still in prison (eleven in all, in August 1914), and others went around in fear of re-arrest under the provisions of the Cat and Mouse

Act; Christabel was in exile in Paris. It was not until 10 August that the Home Secretary, Reginald McKenna, announced that suffragettes, as well as trade unionists who had been convicted of taking part in recent violent strikes, were to be released, 'without solicitation on their part, and without requiring any undertaking from them'; he went on to express the hope that both types of prisoners would 'respond to the feelings of their countrymen and country-women in this time of emergency' and 'be trusted not to stain the causes they have at heart by any further crime or disorder'.

The official WSPU reaction to the war emergency was set out in Mrs Pankhurst's Circular Letter of 13 August 1914. David Morgan, in his book on *Suffragists and Liberals*, quotes only the last part of this letter, and thus fails to bring out the fact that at this stage Mrs Pankhurst was far more preoccupied with the impact of the war crisis on the future of the WSPU than she was with the predicament of the nation as a whole. The letter, therefore, is worth quoting in full.

Dear Friend,
Even the outbreak of war could not affect the action of the WSPU, so long as our comrades were in prison and under torture.

Since their release, it has been possible to consider what should be the course adopted by the WSPU, in view of the war crisis.

It is obvious that even the most vigorous militancy of the WSPU, is for the time being rendered less effective by contrast with the infinitely greater violence done in the present war, not to mere property and economic prosperity alone, but to human life.

As for work for the vote on the lines of peaceful argument, such work is we know, futile even under ordinary conditions, to secure votes for women in Great Britain. How much less, therefore, will it avail at this time of international warfare.

Under all circumstances, it has been decided to economize the Union's energies and financial resources by a temporary suspension of activities. The resumption of active work and the reappearance of the Suffragette, whose next publication will be also temporarily suspended, will be announced when the right time comes.

As a result of the decision announced in this letter, not only shall we save much energy and a very large sum of money, but an opportunity will be given to the Union as a whole, and above all to those individual members who have been in the fighting line to recuperate after the tremendous strain and suffering of the past two years.

As regards the war, the view the WSPU expresses is this:–
We believe that under the joint rule of enfranchised women and men, the nations of the world will, owing to women's influence and authority, find a way of reconciling the claims of peace and honour, and of regulating international relations without bloodshed. We nonetheless believe also that matters having come to the present pass it was inevitable that Great Britain should take part in the war and with that patriotism which has nerved women to endure torture in prison cells for the national good, we ardently desire that our Country shall be victorious – this because we hold that the existence of small nationalities is at stake, and that the status of France and Great Britain is involved.

It will be the future task of women, and only they can perform it, to ensure that the present world tragedy and the peril in which it places civilization, shall not be repeated and therefore, the WSPU will at the first possible moment step forward into the political arena in order to compel the enactment of a measure giving votes to women on the same terms as men.

The letter concludes with a formal paragraph of thanks to WSPU supporters. The letter makes clear that the suspension of activities is due to the upheavals of the immediate crisis, and not because it is thought to be in the national good. It envisages the speedy resumption of suffragette agitation once the immediate war emergency is over (it was, of course, still widely believed that the war would be over by Christmas). Most significant of all is the emphasis placed on the torture endured by suffragettes, and the manner in which, as Mrs Pankhurst sees it, they have been 'in the fighting line'; the present suspension of activities, indeed, will enable the front line warrior to 'recuperate'.[3]

The possibility that suffragettes might still be arrested, despite McKenna's statement, continued for a time to worry the WSPU. Indeed, on 21 August one former suffragette prisoner, Mrs Crowe, was re-arrested, and held by the police for two hours before being released on the direct instructions of the Home Office. Thereafter, the police stuck to the letter of Government policy, and the issue faded away. But another one threatened to come into prominence. On 16 October the Plymouth Watch Committee passed a resolution which suggested that they were in favour of the re-enactment of the Contagious Diseases Acts, providing for the licensing and medical inspection of prostitutes. Immediately, the WSPU began an intensive campaign in Plymouth. All aldermen and all candidates for the local elections, which took place on 2 November, were interviewed. Special interviews took place with the Mayor, the Chief Constable, the Town Clerk and all officials of the Council, and also with all clergy, both conformist and non-conformist, and all doctors. A leading WSPU authority on the subject, Mrs Dacre Fox, insisted on interviews with the Fortress Commander, Major-General Penton, with Captain Norris, in charge of the Fort, with Mrs Scott, wife of the Commander of the Royal Marine Barracks, and also with Miss Soper, one of the heads of the local Salvation Army, the heads of the YMCA and the YWCA, and 'all the influential people of the district, both men and women'. Protest meetings were arranged, and a vigorous correspondence carried on in the local press.[4]

But already the first caginess with which the WSPU had faced the national crisis had passed away. At the beginning of September, Christabel returned to London; there was no longer any danger of her being arrested. A speech to a packed audience of her supporters at the London Opera House on 8 September 1914 raised a number of points which were henceforth to be recurrent themes in the reactions of former suffragettes to the war. First of all, the wickedness of Germany, with its special implications for women: 'Obviously, the might-is-right principle upon which German policy is now based is altogether contrary to the principle upon which women's claim to citizenship depends.' The suffragette issue, and old battles with the politicians were not yet forgotten: the only obstacle to women's franchise in Britain, Christabel maintained, was the 'resistance' to women's 'just demands' by 'a handful of politicians'; Christabel went on to argue that if women had had the vote five years previously, Britain would have been in a proper state of military preparedness for the war with Germany.

The speech then became fixated, as was to happen with many subsequent speeches, on the question of whether women, who spoke of having been in the front line during the suffragette battles, should also be out in the front line in Flanders and France, engaged in real warfare:

> Our position with regard to women fighting is this. If we are needed in the fighting line, we shall be there. If we are needed to attend to the economic prosperity of the country, we shall be there. What it is best in the interests of the State to do, women will do. But it must be clearly understood that if women do not actually take part in the fighting, that argues no inferiority, that argues no diminution of their claim to political equality. It simply means that men and women in co-operation decide the task which, in the interests of the whole, it is most necessary that they shall do. You must remember if the men fight, the women are the mothers. Without the mothers you have no nation to defend. Therefore, we never have admitted – we never shall admit – that even though we do not take part in the actual fighting, we are not equally important from the point of view of citizenship. It is well known that you cannot maintain more than a certain proportion of your citizens in the fighting line. For everyone who fights you must have a number of non-combatants to feed him, to clothe him and to prevent the State for which he is fighting from crumbling into ruins. One thing is certain. You are not now utilizing to the full the activities of women.

This last sentence contained the important cry which increasingly the suffragettes were to take up.

Finally, although she was addressing an audience largely composed of women, Christabel moved into a role in which the Pankhursts were to excel – that of recruiting sergeant.

> We militant women understand so clearly and so well how the man of an age for military service feels at this time. He is wondering if it is really his duty to take his life in his hands and go out to the war. The militants have, at one time or another, had a choice to make which was not so very different from that. It is true that we have never had to face the sudden blow of the enemy which may lay you dead in an instant; but you must remember that, on the other hand, you men who decide to fight have a wonderful backing . . . everybody is supporting you. When we Suffragettes began our fight we had public opinion against us, and, as you all know, that is harder to face than the guns of the enemy.

Then, in the language of Rupert Brooke and thousands of third-rate imitators, she went on to talk of, how, if necessary for the defeat of the enemy, every drop of British blood would be poured out.[5]

The culmination of the transition on the part of Emmeline and Christabel Pankhurst and their followers, from waging war against male obstinacy and weakness to waging war against German wickedness and inciting all British men to go out and take part in that fight, was well symbolized by a meeting held in the Plymouth Guildhall on 17 November at the end of the successful campaign against the suggested re-introduction of the Contagious Diseases Acts. Mrs Dacre Fox, who had spearheaded the campaign, was in the Chair. Now she had other matters on her mind: 'Militant women had gone out prepared to lay down their lives, if necessary, for their cause,' she said. 'Because of their militancy they believed it fitting that they should urge men to be militant in this great fight against the common enemy.' But the speaker people had come to hear was Mrs Pankhurst. She took up immediately the point about

OPPOSITE Recruiting poster 'Women of Britain Say-"Go!" '

30

Published by the PARLIAMENTARY RECRUITING COMMITTEE, London   Poster No. 75   Printed by HILL, SIFFKEN & Co. (L.P.A. Ltd.), Grafton Works, London, N. W. 15741 25 M. 5/15

suffragettes having previously been 'enemies of the Government of this
country', and agreed 'that until this war broke out we were engaged in a
civil war . . . to win from a reluctant Government the citizenship of the
women of this land'. But, she said, 'it was because we love our country so
much that we could not bear to be the serf sex in that country'. The Kaiser
would himself perhaps have been a little surprised by Mrs Pankhurst's
claim that he had taken the suffragette agitation into account when he
decided to launch the war; however, she continued, 'as soon as we were
attacked from outside we agreed to adjourn our quarrels'.

The major part of the speech consisted of a two-fold appeal: an appeal
to women to accept their duty of urging men to flock to the colours; and a
direct appeal to men to 'uphold the honour of the British nation and let us
be proud of you'. A couple of sentences revealed the continuing and
deep-rooted ambivalence in her attitude towards men: 'The war has
made me feel renewed belief in man. It is not that I have ever forgotten the
other side, because as long as there is another side it is our duty to do
what we can to alter it. This war has made me feel how much there is of
nobility in man, in addition to the other thing which we all deplore.'
In speaking passionately of the joys of death – 'to give one's life for one's
country, for a great cause, is a splendid thing' – she was saying nothing
that hundreds of male recruiters in the country were not saying. But the
carrying over of the mystic military imagery of the days of the real, if
limited, suffragette battle into this era of limitless, but, as far as the
suffragettes were concerned, surrogate warfare, is again striking. Mrs
Pankhurst called upon male members of her audience to go into battle
like the knight of old, who knelt before the altar and vowed that he
would keep his sword stainless and with absolute honour to his nation.
If they did this, when they came home they would be able to look British
women in the face, who would then 'have no reason to blush for the
manhood of the nation'. This remark was greeted with great applause.[6]

The coolest reactions to the war emergency were undoubtedly those
of the NUWSS within which Liberal and pacifist sentiment continued to be
strong. The Women's Freedom League at once established the Women's
Suffrage National Aid Corps with the very laudable and practical aim of
providing material assistance to women and children of the poorer
classes. The Nine Elms Settlement set up in August undertook the

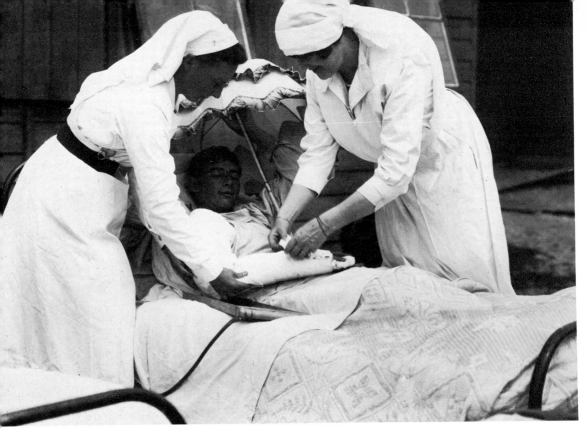

The Duchess of Sutherland attending to a wounded soldier in Calais, July 1917. The Duchess of Sutherland was engaged in organizing medical relief work from August 1914; in October 1914 her first hospital was set up in Dunkirk

distribution of cheap or free milk; but perhaps the vegetarian restaurant which it ran, in reflection of the ideals of Mrs Despard, was less than wholeheartedly welcomed by the poor it was designed to serve. In the East End of London Sylvia Pankhurst's Federation threw itself more devotedly than ever into work for the poor. A pub in the Old Ford Road, 'The Gunmakers Arms', was converted into a canteen and welfare centre called 'The Mothers Arms'.

Probably the vast majority of women shared in the excitement and the quickening of the pulses engendered by the outbreak of war. But the hard facts were of large scale unemployment being caused in many of the women's trades, and of a sharp rise in prices of basic necessities. Part of the trouble lay in the almost inevitable dislocation of normal peace-time trading patterns, the temporary closure of banks, the suspension of credit, the general uncertainty, and the disruption of transport. But another part of it lay in the manner in which upper-class ladies patriotically averted their thoughts from new dresses and fancy hats and thus helped to throw almost half of the women occupied in the millinery, dressmaking and similar trades out of work or on to short-time. Even before the British declaration of war had taken effect the Government had set up a Cabinet Committee on Prevention and Relief of Distress. On 6 August the Prince of Wales issued an appeal for a National Relief Fund; the previous day the Labour Party had set up a War Emergency: Workers' National Committee to watch over the interests of working-class families. People had begun hoarding food during the Bank Holiday weekend that preceded the outbreak of war, and prices had begun to rise then. Within days, bread, the basic foodstuff of the poor, had risen from 5½d (2p) for a 4lb loaf to 8d (3½p) or more.

Many British women earned a precarious living through practising the arts of sewing, knitting, etc. But, as the war was to reveal, many working-class women were not at all skilled in these domestic pursuits; nor, it transpired, were all middle- and upper-class women particularly adept. However, one very widespread female response to the outbreak of war was the knitting of 'comforts' for the troops: socks, waistcoats, helmets, scarves, mitts, and bodybelts. It was said that many men in the trenches used these unwanted, and often unsuitable, items for cleaning their rifles and wiping their cups and plates.

As we have already seen, the professional Queen Alexandra's Imperial Military Nursing Service and the Territorial Force Nursing Services had been augmented by the establishment of the non-professional VADS in 1910: for many girls and women the obvious response to the declaration of war was to enrol as a nurse. 'I spend my time,' a schoolboy reported to his mother, 'being bandaged and unbandaged by the girls who want to be VADS. If some of them ever manage to get into a hospital, heaven help their patients.' At least the novelist Arnold Bennett was gratified: 'This instinct to do something on the part of idle young women or half idle is satisfactory to behold.'

Inciting men to go to war could perhaps also be regarded as a traditional activity to be set alongside knitting and nursing. Certainly the militant suffragettes were far from being the only women to undertake the public work of recruiting for the armies. Recruiting meetings, indoors and outdoors, were addressed by society ladies, famous actresses, and professional beauties. One wonders just what exactly were the true feelings of those music hall stars who mixed an enticing leg-show with recruiting songs, and rounded off the performance by inviting men in the audience to come up on the platform to enlist, rewarding them with a kiss. Doubtless they were as filled with patriotic fervour as anyone else.

War excitement at times came near to hysteria and even derangement, among both men and women. A Dumfriesshire girl began a famous atrocity story by forging a letter which purported to describe how her sister, a nurse in Belgium, had had her breasts cut off by the Germans. Many suffragettes were to the fore in the practice of handing out white

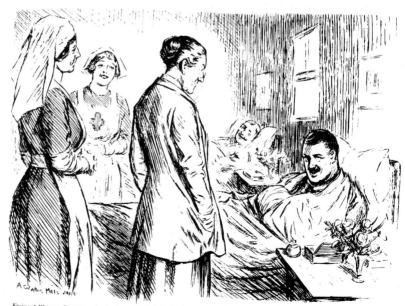

Cartoon probably referring to Dr Louisa Garrett-Anderson at Endell Street Hospital, *Punch* No. 149, 1915

Eminent Woman Surgeon, who is also an ardent Suffragist (to wounded Guardsman). "DO YOU KNOW, YOUR FACE IS SINGULARLY FAMILIAR TO ME. I'VE BEEN TRYING TO REMEMBER WHERE WE'VE MET BEFORE."
Guardsman. "WELL, MUM, BYGONES BE BYGONES. I WAS A POLICE CONSTABLE."

Flower girl throwing roses to wounded soldiers being taken by ambulance from Charing Cross Station

feathers to any young men not wearing military uniform. Non-suffragettes, now only too ready to listen to the exhortations of Emmeline and Christabel Pankhurst, joined in. Wounded soldiers out of uniform were not always exempt from these tender attentions. Again, though, there is no argument that women's reactions were different from, or worse than, men's: the originator of the original white feather scheme was a man, Admiral Penrose-Fitzgerald.

Upper-class Amazons and Distressed Trades

Unemployment in the traditional women's trades continued into 1915, and it was only in May, when the war was beginning to open up a few new job opportunities to women, that the level of women's employment returned to what it had been before the outbreak of war. Men from all walks of life had responded enthusiastically to Lord Kitchener's first recruiting appeal issued on 7 August. By 28 August, in a further appeal, the age limit was raised from 30 to 35, and a special appeal was made to married men. By the middle of September half-a-million of the country's bravest and most idealistic men, not all of them so young, had enlisted. In the early weeks of the war the only official organization responsible for providing allowances and pensions for the wives and children of men on active service was the Commissioners of the Royal Hospital for Soldiers at Chelsea. The actual rates had not changed since the Boer War, and supplementation had to come from charitable funds channelled through the Soldiers' and Sailors' Families Association or from the National Relief Fund. It was the Executive Committee of the latter body which took the decision to raise allowances from 11s 1d (55½p) per week, with 1s 9d for each child, to 12s 6d with 2s for each child; these rates, with a further slight increase in the child's allowance, were officially adopted by the Government on 1 October. As it was discovered that in a large number of cases soldiers were not in fact married to the women they were living with, the Executive Committee decided that 'where there was evidence that a real home had been maintained allowances should be made to unmarried mothers and their children'. Here was the first swallow in the migration from older moral standards which was to take place during the war. Even when allowances were established as due, there were often outrageously long delays before payment was made. Many families were in dire straits.

Prices continued to escalate. In February 1915 flour was 75 per cent dearer than it had been a year before; meat (still something of a luxury for poor families) 6–12 per cent up; sugar 72 per cent up; and coal 15 per cent up. Labour members in Parliament stated that many labourers were getting only one good meal a week; they did not say whether the labourers' wives or children were getting even that.

Many titled ladies, and other upper-class figures, responded to the example set by the Prince of Wales's Appeal and started their own charities for families in difficulties caused by the war. One group of ladies established the National Milk Hostels Committee to supply milk from their own home farms to distressed families; characteristically, a thorough investigation of need was carried out before the milk was made available. The Cabinet Committee already mentioned set up a Central Committee on Women's Employment which was able to do useful work since, apart from the usual titled ladies, it contained among its membership Margaret Bondfield and another Labour party member, the woman doctor, Marion Phillips; most important, the secretary of the Committee was Mary Macarthur. Mary Macarthur insisted that the various local sub-committees should include 'a strong representation of women from working-class industrial organizations'. Yet even on this committee the heavily patronizing attitudes of the time towards working women were all too apparent.

The basic function of the Committee was to draw up various schemes for the employment of women; it was firmly laid down that these schemes were to be open only to women formerly in employment, now thrown out of work by the war, and not the wives of men who were themselves thrown out of work. Four schemes were undertaken: first, training women workers in trades for which new export opportunities were opening up (this was almost pure optimism; in wartime such openings were practically non-existent); secondly, training in skilled trades in which there was normally a shortage of labour, for example, machinists; thirdly, training in domestic economy, especially cooking; and fourthly, production of 'useful articles' for Poor Law Hospitals and maternity wards, such as clothing, nightdresses, bedjackets, knitted garments for babies, and cheap cradles.

The minimum rate of pay in these schemes was set at 3d per hour (to give some kind of idea of the relative value of such figures, it could be noted that canteen dinners provided under the same scheme were offered at cost price, which also worked out at exactly 3d). The maximum working week was to be 40 hours, and in allocating the exact number of hours to be worked, and, indeed, in choosing which women were to be employed under this scheme, family income was to be taken into account. Nothing in the operation of the scheme was to be allowed to interfere with the course of ordinary trade: the 'useful articles' produced under the scheme were not to be offered for sale 'but would be given through the Local Representative Committee or other approved sources, to persons who had no purchasing power'. More than this it was decided that every article produced should be 'stamped in such a way as to identify its origin and pawnbrokers should be circularized with a warning notice against accepting articles so stamped in pawn'.[7]

The main 'workroom' operated by the Committee was 'The Depot' at 12 Park Street in Southwark. The atmosphere of the whole operation can best be conveyed by quoting this letter about work at the Depot written by Margaret Bondfield to Mary Macarthur on 13 January 1915 and including extracts from the reports supplied to Margaret Bondfield by her forewomen:

From December 28 to January 1 inclusive, we had a most interesting time in the workroom. The women had each a piece of coloured material given to them, out of which they each made an article which they were allowed to keep. This seemed only fairly interesting to them, the real zeal began when they started mending their own clothes. Two pairs of old stockings quickly made one pair of new. Mother's (past repairing) skirt, a new one for a girl; Father's old trousers, made little Johnny a tidy boy. I examined the skirts of the women, the majority of them were in a most deplorable condition. Orders: '*All skirt bottoms to be repaired*'. Some of them looked very crestfallen. At last it came out – 'We aint got no others to wear while them as we have got on are mended, but can we take 'em off?' The women seemed anxious to be tidy, so off they came and the ragged pieces cut off neatly, turned up and bound with braid. One woman asked 'Could she take her petticoat off and mend it? I did wash it last night and it's the only one I got.'

The majority of blouses and aprons were held together with pins, these are now replaced with hooks and eyes and buttons. Many a child has returned to school this week minus one thing – tattered underclothing. They could not understand why they were not allowed to patch and darn their own clothes in their own way, but when the patches were finished the proper way they saw the improvement.[8]

Upper-class women, with their long tradition of supporting their men in the task of maintaining their authority, not only in Britain but over the vast tracts of the British Empire, entered enthusiastically into many other voluntary activities apart from welfare work. Welcoming Belgian refugees, and finding suitable accommodation for them in accordance with their social class, was the preoccupation of many society ladies at the beginning of the war. However, there were tougher tasks which women of the right social status could allocate to themselves. From the early weeks of the war, right through to the end of 1916, quite a number of different uniformed women's organizations were formed, each an odd,

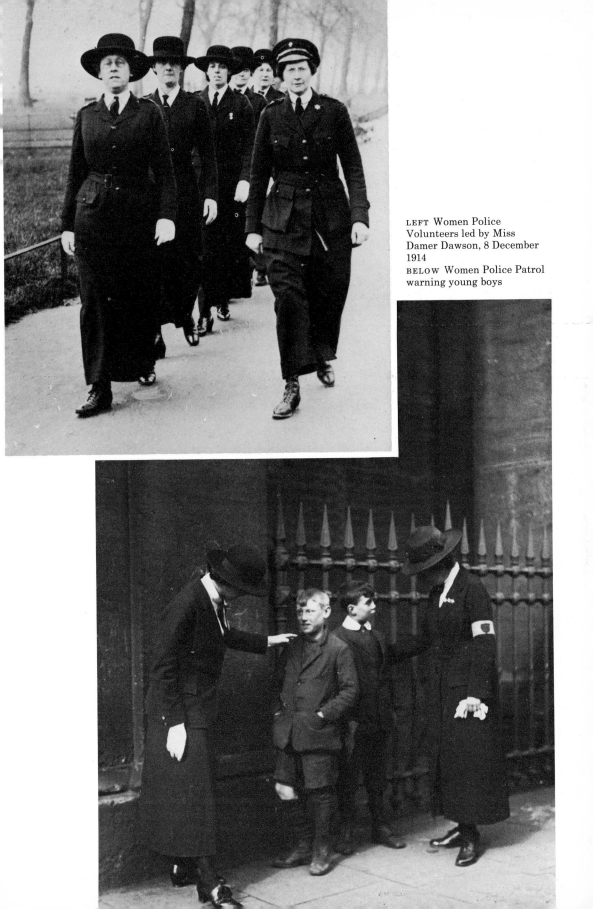

LEFT Women Police Volunteers led by Miss Damer Dawson, 8 December 1914
BELOW Women Police Patrol warning young boys

but not necessarily ineffective mixture of Girl Guides, County Charity, and Territorial Army. First in the field were the Women's Emergency Corps, founded by The Hon. Evelina Haverfield, the Women's Volunteer Reserve, sponsored by the Marchioness of Londonderry, the Marchioness of Titchfield, and the Countess of Pembroke and Montgomery, and Mrs Dawson Scott's Women's Defence Relief Corps. The khaki uniforms and felt hats which The Volunteer Reserve women designed for themselves provided the basic model for the various women's auxiliary corps subsequently set up. One survivor of these early days has left us with this account:

> I was 16 years of age and my twin brother . . . enlisted in the Army as 19 years old, so I enlisted in the 'Womens Defence Relief Corps' in Wallasey. We were trained by an elderly Segt in the Cheshire Regt: i.e.: – Voice drill, military and Swedish drill, semaphor signalling and shooting. I won my cross guns.[9]

Each organization had behind it one, or at most two or three strong-willed women. Their motives seem to have consisted of: a genuine desire to help the National effort, a liking for uniform, an urge to boss other people around, and a passion to compete with anyone else who had had the temerity to set up an organization of their own. Single-minded professional purpose was most evident in the Women's Hospital Corps formed in September by Dr Flora Murray and Dr Louisa Garrett Anderson, who dressed their members in a greenish-grey uniform with small cloth caps trimmed with veils. It took the War Office till April 1915 to recognize formally the role, albeit a limited one, which these women's organizations could play in releasing soldiers for combatant duties. As a force essentially designed for colonial warfare, the British army was based on the principle that it must be totally self-contained, with soldiers themselves being responsible for cooking and other support tasks. Now the most important of the voluntary women's organizations came into being, the Women's Legion, organized by the redoubtable Lady Londonderry who had important political connections. Yet the first women recruited as army cooks for certain convalescent camps were obtained by the usual methods for engaging domestic servants. The Women's Legion, organized into Canteen, Ambulance, and Cookery sections, was officially recognized by an Army Council Instruction of February 1916. Meantime the War Office had instituted the Women's Forage Corps which substituted for soldiers in home camps in all matters to do with the distribution of feeding stuffs for horses.

Much nearer the core of the social experience of the majority of women were the special police functions assumed by members of the National Union of Women Workers – essentially, it must be remembered, a body led by middle- and upper-class women. On 2 September 1914 an emergency meeting of the Rescue and Preventive Sectional Committee of the NUWW was called to consider 'grave rumours of uncontrolled excitement, and undesirable conduct of women and girls (some of them almost children) in the neighbourhood of Camps, Recruiting Offices, and other places where men were stationed or frequent'.[10] The NUWW women patrols were given official recognition by a Home Office circular of 29 October 1914. Already (naturally!) a rival body was in the field, The Women's Police Volunteers, organized by Miss Nina Boyle, with Miss Damer Dawson as chief officer. This body was the first to achieve a major success, when at the end of November two uniformed women police volunteers began work in Grantham, where an enormous military camp had been set up. Even more

Woman vet removing shoe from horse

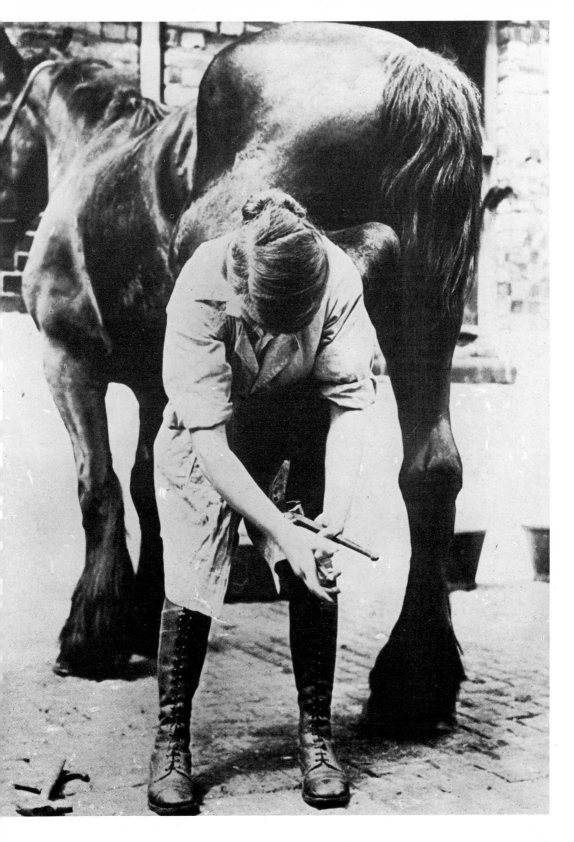

naturally, in February 1915 Miss Damer Dawson left the Women's Police Volunteers, and started up the Women's Police Service.

One rare, and potentially invaluable, quality which some upper-class women possessed, was access to, and ability to drive, that new toy, the motorcar. The first organization to appear, at the end of the year, The Volunteer Motor Mobilization Corps, was founded by a man, and staffed by both men and women. This voluntary organization, too, gained the sanction and approval of the War Office. Motivations and morals, are made apparent by two statements: 'The names of owners who lend cars will be published weekly in the press'; and 'chauffeurs are strictly instructed that under no circumstances whatever should they stop at or upon licensed premises'. Most intriguing of all these organizations, in name at least, is the Almeric Paget Military Massage Corps. On the outbreak of the war Mr and Mrs Almeric Paget offered the medical authorities at the War Office to supply and run a Corps of 50 fully trained masseuses for work among the wounded in the United Kingdom. The offer was accepted, and appointments of the masseuses to hospitals began in September 1914. Early in 1915 the Corps was given official recognition. In January 1917, just to continue the story of this fascinating outfit, the first masseuses (56 in number) were sent over to France. Altogether, the total numbers in the Corps were: in January 1916, 900; in January 1917, 1,200; in January 1918, 1,500; and on Armistice Day 1918, 2000.

First Aid Nursing Yeomanry, showing FANYs and their ambulance. FANY had established a motor mechanic training scheme in the prewar period

Whatever Happened to the Suffragettes?

Emmeline and Christabel Pankhurst had moved far towards making national propaganda and recruitment to the Armed Forces their basic objectives, to the neglect of the suffrage issue. However, it would be quite wrong to write them off as contributors to the cause of women's rights; in fact a close scrutiny of their speeches, and of the pages of their newspaper *Suffragette* (from when it reappeared in April 1915 till when it changed its name to *Britannia* in October 1915), shows that for all their hysteria, and all their eccentricity, they still had a good grasp of some of the essential features of the women's case, extending beyond the mere question of winning the vote.

In her first speech on returning to London, Christabel had made two very interesting points, one in relation to the women's movement, the other in relation to social policy generally. First, she hammered home the point that married women ought to have an income of their own.

> How often have we told you that if you want the country to be
> prosperous, you must organize and utilize the productive energy
> of women as well as of men, so that they may not be in a position of
> being a burden to the country! Why is it that every woman who
> wants to earn her living, and is physically fit to do so, has not a
> trade in her fingers, so that she could step into the place that her
> husband leaves vacant, or pursue some occupation of her own? It is
> a serious weakness to our country that women should be
> economically dependent upon others.

A second point was that the whole nation should be put on food rations 'as the soldiers are'; Christabel had long lost touch with her former Labour associates, but on this issue of food she put the rhetorical question, 'if there are to be no class distinctions at the Front, why should there be class distinctions at home where the question of bread and butter is concerned?' A soldier, of course, could have told her of the different messing conditions of officers and men which showed that class distinctions were very far from being ignored at the Front.

Emmeline devoted more and more of her attentions to the question of employment of women in the national interest, and began to work closely with Lloyd George, who until May 1915 was Chancellor of the Exchequer in the Liberal Government. Christabel, on the other hand, was increasingly used as a propagandist. The British Government was specially anxious to secure the good opinion and, if possible, the active military involvement of the United States. Thus Christabel delivered two famous speeches at The Carnegie Hall, New York, on 24 October 1914 and on 30 January 1915.[11] In the first of these speeches she remarked that: 'Bismarck boasted that Germany is a male nation. We do not want male nations . . . the more you have the man's and the woman's point of view balanced, the more sane will be the nation, the more just and wise will be the nation.' Perhaps because of her own fixation on the question of women's military role, she seemed to completely misunderstand a question put to her about Joan of Arc and 'the cosmopolitan spirit of justice, democracy and brotherhood'; instead of talking about cosmopolitanism and brotherhood (which, the questioner presumably meant, were being violated by Britain's participation in the war), Christabel reacted to the Joan of Arc image:

> If we are needed to fight, we shall be ready for it. We are not
> afraid. But, as Mr Lloyd George said – and he was right too, for
> once – those who stay at home, those who suffer the agony of

anxiety as to the fate of those dear to them, they are not playing the easiest part by any means. Think what it means to the wife and the mother to stay at home and know what the one who is dear to her is suffering at the Front! The women are, indeed, the greatest sufferers in time of war. So it is not fear that holds us back; it is the interests of the nation which weighs with us.

It involves no denigration of women's role in peace and in war to remark that this equation of women's sufferings at home with the sordid hellishness and desperate danger of the trenches borders on the outrageous.

Like many passionate natural speakers, Christabel had great gifts of humour. During her second Carnegie Hall address she was heckled about the British Navy, seen by many Americans as in itself a major threat to world peace. Christabel handled her hecklers in the following manner which brought tremendous laughter and applause: 'I like these interruptions. But I will tell you, Sir, this: if you were a Suffragette, you would have been thrown out and then, after you had been thrown out, I should have said I didn't believe in your violent methods.' She then got in a nice appeal to American sentiment by reminding her audience that they had had their Revolutionary war, adding, with great effect, though less historical accuracy, that that had been 'a war between a German King in England and British people over here'.

Christabel was not the only British supporter of women's suffrage to tour the United States. A week before her first meeting in the Carnegie Hall, Mrs Emmeline Pethick-Lawrence had addressed a packed audience on the question of internationalism and the need for concluding a negotiated peace as quickly as possible. The women's Suffrage Movement in the United States was largely pacifist in outlook, and it was mainly through the initiative of American women that a proposal was put forward in December for a Women's Peace Conference to be held at The Hague on neutral Dutch territory. Despite the canny course pursued by Mrs Fawcett, this proposal caused a crisis in the ranks of the NUWSS. Mrs Fawcett came out strongly against the sending of NUWSS delegates to the Conference arguing that 'women are as subject as men are to national prepossessions and susceptibilities, and it would hardly be possible to bring together the women of the belligerent countries without violent bursts of anger'. But at the meeting of the National Council of the NUWSS in February 1915, the first to be held since the outbreak of war, all the office bearers except Mrs Fawcett and the Treasurer resigned, together with ten members of the Executive Committee. For all that, Mrs Fawcett, who was much more closely in touch with the temper of the country and its womenfolk, sailed on triumphantly, devoting more and more of her energies to the questions of women's employment, training, and conditions of work. She also gave attention to the possible threat of a German invasion.

The experience of France and Belgium shows, on the one hand, what the horrors of invasion are amidst an unorganized population, and on the other, how much can be done to mitigate these horrors when women take responsibility, and have control of the situation. We believe that if women organized themselves beforehand to look after the sick, the aged, young girls, and children, either in the event of invasion or occupation, the whole business could be infinitely better conducted, than if the women are left to carry out instructions which may or may not be wise, but which will have been issued without their advice or co-operation.[12]

Common Cause said little to nothing now about the Suffrage issue as such. Indeed, the organ which continued to argue the women's case most forcefully and persuasively was *Votes for Women*, and then many of its articles were written by men, which is perhaps why they sometimes had a rather supercilious and patronizing tone.

Many of those women who disagreed with Mrs Fawcett played an important and honourable role in supporting the anti-war cause and, later, the cause of the Conscientious Objectors. As Clifford Allen, Fenner Brockway, and the other young leaders of the No-Conscription Fellowship disappeared into prison, they were first replaced by older men beyond conscription age; when these men too were imprisoned for their anti-conscription activities, it was young women who took over and effectively ran the No-Conscription Fellowship on behalf of the men. Under the inspired leadership of the former NUWSS Council member, Catherine Marshall, a whole wilderness of suffragist and suffragette subleties and stratagems were deployed on behalf of the persecuted and widely detested 'conchies'.

Sylvia Pankhurst, to the deep chagrin of her mother, who regretted that there was no way of preventing Sylvia from using the name of 'Pankhurst', together with her newly re-christened Workers' Suffrage Federation, also maintained a resolute opposition to the war. Of course there were cranks among women pacifists as there were among men pacifists. In a famous trial held in March 1917, an anarchist second-hand clothes dealer from Derby, Mrs Alice Wheeldon, whose real crimes were the sheltering of deserters and conscientious objectors and a vociferous general hostility to the Government, was accused of plotting with her daughter and son-in-law to kill Lloyd George and Arthur Henderson (a leading Labour politician) by means of poisoned darts. It is clear from reports of the case that the police had made use of *agent provocateurs*, and it was on the most dubious evidence that Mrs Wheeldon was sentenced to ten years' penal servitude, her married daughter to five years, and her son-in-law to seven years; the other daughter, Harriet, was discharged (perhaps for 'co-operating' with the police).

The bent towards physical action which had always been a characteristic of the suffragettes (how much, indeed, of their pre-war violence had simply been due to frustration over being prevented from fulfilling themselves in complete and active lives?) showed itself in the way in which they seized upon many of the rather scarce job opportunities which were opening up in the first phase of the war. However, in one rather amusing echo of the pre-war quarrels among women themselves, the Women Police Patrols sponsored by the respectable NUWW decided that it could scarcely recruit suffragettes who had been inside His Majesty's prisons.

It was not till March 1915 that the Government announced that it was compiling a register of women willing to do industrial, agricultural or clerical work. Although 40,000 women registered immediately, in fact little work was found for them. Two experienced women from the clerical staff of the Glasgow Tramways Department were in April taken on as the first tram conductresses in the country. In general it was very much a case on the one hand of imaginative enterprise on the part of employers, on the other of individual initiative on the part of women themselves. Often it was simply a case of a woman taking over the job vacated by her husband, running a shop or a small business for instance, or of women or girls helping out in a family concern because of the shortage of outside male labour. One lady remembers:

Married woman carrying on her husband's chimney sweeping work

45

LEFT Woman assisting
village blacksmith
(probably her husband)

I was born in a small village called Four Mile Bridge, near
Holyhead, Anglesey – one of a family of eleven – seven girls and
four boys – myself being the second daughter. My father was a
blacksmith, working hard to keep his large family. During the 'Great
War' when the few farmers were called up there were no strikers
(can't think of a better word) to make the horses' shoes so at the age
of sixteen I did all the striking, and between us, we both managed to
keep the Smithy open . . . At the time I was studying for my
matriculation at the Holyhead Grammer School, which meant that
the horses' shoes had to be made very early morning before cycling
the five miles to the school. We usually managed to make eight shoes
and father could then get on with the shoeing, during the day.[13]

The resentment of women who felt that they were not being given the
opportunity to contribute to the national effort was only one element of a
feeling which was gathering strength in April 1915 that the Asquith
Liberal Government was not rising to the full needs of total war. This
feeling was to culminate in the political crisis of May 1915, which resulted
in the replacement of the Asquith Liberal Government by a National
Coalition Government, still, however, headed by Asquith. As always,
some of the women's feelings seemed to be slightly ambivalent. One letter
written in reply to the Government's call for women to register contained
a request for work as a docker, together with the writer's conviction that
all dock labourers ought to be at the Front and their places taken by
women.[14]

LEFT Women railway
ticket collectors

BELOW Two ticket collectors:
the old man and the young
woman, an increasingly usual
image during the War

Rather more progress was already being made in the genteel clerical employments where it was accepted as fairly natural that growth in the number of women employed should take place. The National Provincial and Union Bank of England Limited employed the first woman teller in September 1914. The Atlas Assurance Company Limited declared that: 'Ladies were employed by this Company for many years before the War as Typists only. Their employment to replace our permanent Staff on active service commenced in November 1914.' The Allied Assurance Company reported that it had been employing women since 1903 but not 'to any large extent' till 1915.[15] In fact, the statistics show 1915 as the important year of expansion in clerical and commercial employment for women, setting it apart from almost all other jobs, where the major developments were still to come.

RIGHT London bus conductress; women were not taken on until the early summer of 1916

ABOVE Woman tram driver at Lowestoft; there was much resistance from the men and by the end of the War there was still only a handful of women drivers

CHAPTER THREE

THE
TURNING POINTS

MUNITIONS AND CONSCRIPTION

May 1915 to Autumn 1916

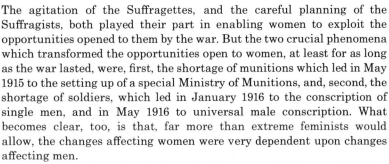

The Shell Shortage

The agitation of the Suffragettes, and the careful planning of the Suffragists, both played their part in enabling women to exploit the opportunities opened to them by the war. But the two crucial phenomena which transformed the opportunities open to women, at least for as long as the war lasted, were, first, the shortage of munitions which led in May 1915 to the setting up of a special Ministry of Munitions, and, second, the shortage of soldiers, which led in January 1916 to the conscription of single men, and in May 1916 to universal male conscription. What becomes clear, too, is that, far more than extreme feminists would allow, the changes affecting women were very dependent upon changes affecting men.

Shortly after the outbreak of war the Government had secured a rather vague 'industrial truce' from the trade unions. This was followed by a number of conferences in which the Government sought to get trade union approval for what, revealingly, was called 'dilution': this meant the placing of semi-skilled or unskilled men in jobs formerly reserved for skilled men, and, of course, the placing of women in jobs formerly reserved for men. By May 1915 practically nothing had been achieved in the way of bringing women into male industrial occupations, and there had, in fact, only been a small increase in the number of women doing unskilled work in the various existing munitions factories. It was in May that the Asquith Liberal Government was rocked by a major political crisis, fundamentally a product of discontent generated by the rather lax way in which the war effort was being conducted, but above all by the revelation of the way in which British troops were being handicapped by a shortage of high explosives. The new Government included the Conservative leaders, Arthur Henderson, Secretary of the Labour Party, and it had a Minister of Munitions, none other than Lloyd George. The new Ministry of Munitions took over direct control of certain factories exclusively concerned with war production, it began to build its own State-owned factories, together with special accommodation for workers, and it exercised control over certain jobs relating to munitions production in factories which were not exclusively devoted to this: in these three spheres the Ministry could legally enforce the suspension of trade union practices, which had sometimes served as a barrier to the employment of women, and it could directly encourage the recruitment of women.

It is true that Lloyd George had also established a working relationship with Mrs Pankhurst. Lloyd George was good at gaining the favour of potentially powerful individuals in the field of what is usually described public opinion. Just as Lord Northcliffe's *Daily Mail* tended to follow a line favourable to Lloyd George, and also, be it said, to a vigorous prosecution of the war, and unfavourable to Asquith, so when *Suffragette*

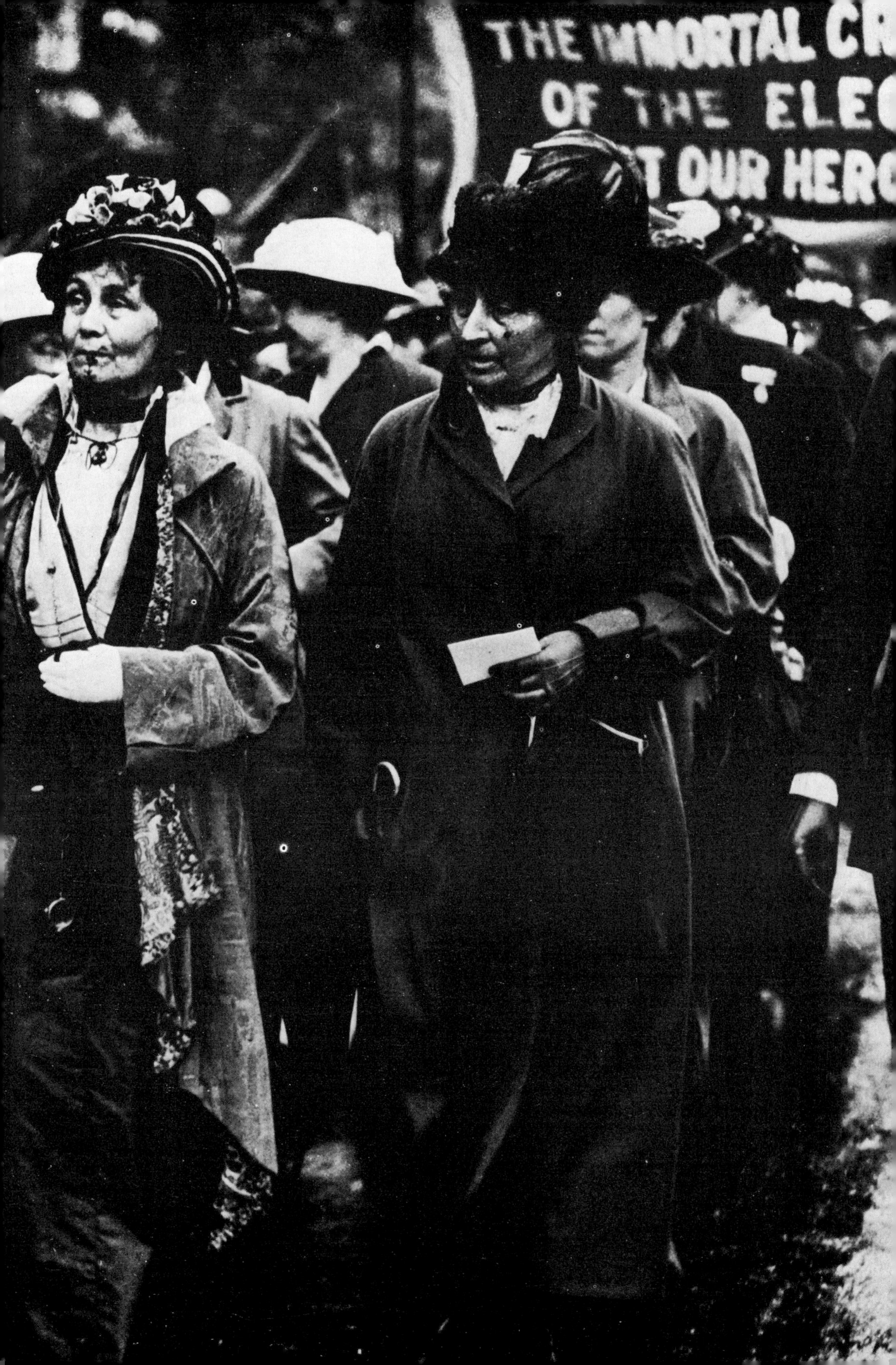
THE IMMORTAL CR
OF THE ELEC
OUR HERO

It would be tedious to describe all the regulations which were promul-
gated in regard to the status of women in the munitions factories; and,
indeed, one male trade unionist on a deputation to the Ministry in June
1917 said that it would take a good lawyer to work out the meaning of all
the regulations, and that certainly he and his colleagues could not
understand them. Mention should however be made of the famous circular
'L2' of 28 October 1915, which almost became part of First World War
folklore, as the basis of all regulations concerning the remuneration of
munition workers. In theory the conditions as they evolved seem broadly
fair. Women doing 'men's work' were to be paid not less than 6d per hour
with a minimum of 24s per week. Women replacing semi-skilled men were
to be paid according to the nature of the work and the ability of the women.
Women replacing fully skilled tradesmen were 'in all cases to be paid as
from commencement the time rates of the tradesmen whose work they
undertake'. However, there was a let-out, which could be exploited to
women's disadvantage: 'A woman shall be considered as not employed
on the work customarily done by fully skilled tradesmen, but a part only
thereof, if she does not do the customary setting up or, where there is no
setting up, if she requires skilled supervision to a degree beyond that
customarily required by fully skilled tradesmen undertaking the work in
question.'[16] By unnecessarily keeping women in this, as it were, position
of tutelage, employers could pay them considerably less than the rate
for a male skilled worker. However, it was categorically laid down that
piece-work rates would be the same for women as for men. In many ways
the Ministry had a clearer field when dealing with the area of 'women's
work', for here the regulations really did mean that women undertaking
the same sort of unskilled work that they had done before the war were
now being far better paid for it.

Although later in the war men at the Front were often upset by
rumours that conscription for women was about to be imposed, there
never was any conscription for women during the First World War. Yet
some women, looking back through the hazy mists of memory, do write of
having been 'called up'. The position was that both in the various voluntary schemes, and then in Government schemes such as the National
Factories, Women's Forage Corps, and, later, the Land Army, women were
required to go through a form of 'enlistment', signing a definite contract
committing themselves for six months, or a year's service. In factories
they were constrained by the system of 'leaving certificates', which was
also a great grievance to male trade unionists: no worker could move
from one employment to another connected with munitions, unless he had
a leaving certificate from the previous employer.

ABOVE Girls working in a
shell-filling factory, wearing
respirators
LEFT Filling exploder bags
with TNT, Woolwich Arsenal.
The health precautions are
supervised by Miss Lilian
Barker, the celebrated lady
superintendent of the Royal
Arsenal, Woolwich, where she
was appointed in December
1915 with her staff

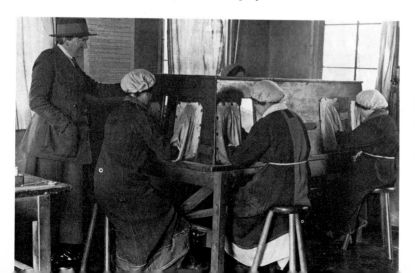

Some of the women who came into the new munitions factories were from the textile industry where organization along trade union lines did exist, or from other branches of the metal trades where there were sometimes opportunities for joining a trade union. But, in the words of Miss C. V. Butler of the Historical Records Branch, 'they came also from Scotch fishing villages, from Irish bogs, and the workrooms and villas of English provincial towns'.[17] Such women had no experience at all of industrial organization and trade union bargaining.

Only munitions factories were formally under Government control, but the Government and Local Authorities participated in appeals which other private employers might make for women labour. In the cases of the more adventurous and active young women we find that during the war they moved in and out of different types of employment, sometimes for one of the voluntary semi-military corps, sometimes for private

OVERLEAF Interior of a howitzer shop

'Munitions Workers' Patriotic
Procession', 23 July 1916

employers, sometimes in Government-sponsored munitions scheme
Entirely in keeping with the attitudes of the time, there was still muc
overlap between private initiative and official initiative. On 19 July 191
Lady Moir and Lady Cowan established at Lesney House, Erith, Kent,
scheme for training leisured ladies to do weekend work at Vicker
Armaments factory at Erith. Eventually many of the leisured ladies move
on to doing a full week's work. The first skilled women workers in
privately owned munitions factory were those who began at Sir Willia
Beardmore's Engineering Works in Glasgow in June 1915. The idea c
training upper-class ladies for part-time work was extended to this factor
in November 1915. At this stage, in 1915, often the idea of establishin
crèches at factories to enable married women with small children t
work, came from private individuals.

Munitionettes and Others

Having provided these rather dry general outlines, I must now try to fi
in the human detail of one or two individual experiences. Among th
papers collected by the Women's War Work Committee is a fascinatin
personal autobiographical account of the triumphs and tribulations of a
educated, independent-minded woman launched into the male world o
the factory floor; since it was actually written up in 1919 it has a specia
value as an authentic source. It also derives a special edge and piquanc
from the writer's strongly conservative attitudes and hostility to trad
unionists and pacifists:

On 2 Jan. 1916 I began my munitions training course, which lasted
four weeks. The alternatives at that time, so far as I could ascertain
them, were a technical schools course, lasting from six to eight
weeks costing 2/6 a week; or the class I attended, which was run by
the London Society for Women's Suffrage lasting from four to six
weeks, costing 10/6 a week. (Very different to the later encourage-
ments of free training and maintenance allowance.) The course was
much the same in both cases, being the fitting course, which with
modifications and additions, was taught at all technical schools all
through the war, together with two or three turning exercises.

Even the short hours worked at this class were a very considerable
strain, and the girls came off the unaccustomed three hour shift
looking just as drawn as they did off a five hour shift later on. For
myself I found the muscular strain worse than the standing and
fatigue, and it was weeks before the stiffness wore off – stiffness that
made every muscle tender to the touch.

In February I became an employee at Messrs G's aero-engine works
near London. I had the fortune to get into a small workshop quite
distinct from the rest of the works, where a small auxiliary part of
the engine was to be made, and which was to be run by women as far
as possible. At first there were only the manager, two men and five
girls including myself, but before I left the number of girls had been
increased to about twenty.

Mr M. the manager, hoped to be able to employ only educated
girls, though this proved to be impossible, especially later on. But
several came from the training class which I had attended, and there
was always a large enough proportion that the atmosphere of our
shop was quite different from that of the rest of the works. For we
were most of us 'out' to learn all we could, and to get through as
much work as possible, which could hardly be said of the average
munition worker.

Conditions at G's were not ideal in those days. It was an old established firm that was increasing at a great rate, and they took on a considerable number of women, although there was quite inadequate accommodation for them. The only cloak room for women was that in our shop, and the consequent crowding was a great discomfort. It meant that all classes came to our shop, too, and there were continual complaints of thefts.

Hours were 7.00 a.m. till 12.00, 1.00 till 5.30 p.m. and overtime 6.00 to 8.00 p.m. Overtime was called optional, and in our shop was so for many months, but later it became customary though not really compulsory. A quarter of an hour for tea at 4.00 p.m. was very soon given to the women, and later another quarter for lunch in the middle of the morning. But such was our zeal for work that some of us worked right through the lunch quarter instead of going to the canteen. (The state of our resources, too, did not admit of extra meals.) There was a crowded canteen served by voluntary workers. Food was of course rough and roughly served, and men and women shared the same canteen. I, and most of the others in my shop, lived close by and always went home to dinner.

We found the cold in the shops intense that winter, as warming apparatus was very inadequate, and coke buckets which were added only warm a small circle, and fill the whole shop with fumes which add insult to injury.

But while speaking of conditions I must add that before I left in April 1917, things had changed considerably. The canteen was enlarged and run on more business-like lines while meals being served in relays prevented overcrowding; a large cloak room had been built for the women, and hot water laid on; steam fed radiators had been put on in the shops, stools were supplied to the girls, a 'welfare supervisor' had been appointed; and a rest room built. Red Cross work which had originally been done by one of the clerks in the pay office, was put in charge of two trained nurses on day and night shifts. These changes and improvements are, of course, only such as were going on all over the country in 1916 and 1917.

In the matter of pay we fared badly at G's. New hands began with 15/– for four weeks unless they had attended a course of training of some sort in which case they received £1 – i.e. $4\frac{1}{2}$d an hour for a $53\frac{1}{4}$ hour week. This was the standard rate of pay for women, and was supposed to be only augmented by piece work prices. But in our shop there was no piece work for months because there was no output, and one girl at any rate received this pay for six months. For myself, I had understood there would be rises, and when I found this was not so I gave notice, as I could not possibly live on £1 a week. I was then offered another penny an hour which I accepted, although it was impossible to make ends meet even with this. By the time I left I had worried 8d an hour out of Mr M. and he admitted I had been worth more than I had been getting all the way along.

We were all of us content to put up with the bad pay for the sake of the conditions. We felt that we might go further and fare very much worse. We all got on well together, the shop was large and light and airy, and no manager could have been more considerate to work under.

There was considerable discontent about money all through the works, because of the inequality of piece work prices. If a job had been a man's job, the price set on it was based on a man's rate of pay, and a woman put on to it would earn £3 or £4; whereas the price set on what was originally a woman's job was based on her rate of pay and she made a total averaging 28/- or 30/-, and though these inequalities became more level as time went on, I heard that in 1918 the Milling Section were still the best paid, as they had been in 1916, although the work was neither so skilled or so responsible as some of the other sections and this because it was some time before women were put on to the work.

As for the work itself – I have said that we were making a small accessory for an aero-engine. This part had progressed not much further than blue prints when I first joined the shop, having never been constructed, tested, or passed by the Admiralty.

For the first few months the work was mostly tool making – tool holders for two small turret lathes, mandrels, cutters, arbors, gauges of many sorts, templates, jigs, etc. besides the turning of some of the more straightforward parts, washers, distance washers, spindles, gudgeon pins etc. But soon castings began to arrive and we were able to start on casings, cylinders, pistons and so on. At first there were only a few lathes, two small turret lathes, a sensitive drill, and a universal grinder in the shop; but soon a milling machine was added, and other lathes and capstans, and new hands were taken on as fast as the machinery was set up. I was the only one with a preference for bench work, and though I did some turning at first I very soon had enough to occupy me at other things. At first, too, I was the only operator of the milling machine, as there was no repetition work ready for it; and I had also always to set up and test any new set of cutters on the turrets and capstans. For the rest my work consisted of cutter shaping and fitting, jig making, and various simple tool-fitting jobs. If work was slack I shaped and hardened a stock of tools for the turners.

Later when we began to turn out work, there was of course much less tool-fitting to do, and I was given all the viewing and assembling. The latter included a good deal of drilling and tapping and some nice filing. The only repetition work I had was the hobbing of certain gear wheels that we used – not a nice job, as the gear was not adjustable, and it was difficult to steer between jamming and too much back-lash. I also had certain pinions to harden. We used to send them to the hardening shop, but they always came back warped so we did them ourselves. Before I left I had three girls working under me at viewing, fitting and assembling.

Mr M. was always much interested in our work, and would take endless pains to teach anyone who was ready to learn, and even allowed me a voice in the designing of jigs. Without his teaching I could not possibly have done the work I did do.

But I thought it better to leave at the end of a year, as I felt that I was capable of either more skilled work, or of supervising more than three girls, and though there was talk of giving me a better job in the works it never materialized, and at the end of fourteen months, April 1917, I left and was taken on to the staff of the Ministry of Munitions as a 'Demonstrator Operative'.

As Demonstrator Operative I was sent to Messrs A, a firm just outside London, as tool fitter. Here I was to establish the fact, for the benefit to foreman and tool-room hands, that a woman was capable of doing skilled work. It was a position fraught with con-siderable nerve strain as the manager and foreman only knew my real position – to my fellow men I was one of themselves, and as the shop was socialist to a man of the Bolshevist type with a large sprinkling of conscientious objectors and pro-Germans, had it been known that I was drawing Government pay, I think I should have been roughly handled. And as such things can never be kept secret for long, a factory being a hot-bed of gossip, I never felt secure.

This was a large factory, and though many hundreds of women were employed, they only did factory repetition work, and I was such a matter of interest to the whole community that there was a stream of sight-seers through the shop the first few days (there was no discipline). Here conditions were very different from those I had left, though I felt the want of companions more than anything else. Cloakrooms were crowded, noisy, dirty and worse than dirty; the yard was impassable in wet weather and had to be bridged with planks; the tool room was close and badly lighted; the canteen was pandemonium; the food was unpalatable, (but that I ate it I should say uneatable) and I could obtain no rooms nearer than twenty five minutes walk, which made dinner in the canteen a necessity.

The tool-room hours were 7.30 a.m. to 1.00 p.m. and 2.00 p.m. till 8.00 p.m. Saturdays till 6.00 p.m. There were no intervals for lunch and tea, though tea could be sent for from the canteen and drunk standing. These hours are of course longer than those laid down for women in the Factory and Workshops Act, but I was unaware of this at the time, and in any case I knew that women as a class were being sampled in me, not only for their work, but for their behaviour, time-keeping, endurance, and general adaptability, and had I known it I should have done nothing to have them shortened.

My work at first was the making of several drilling jigs; sets of extractors for presses; various repairing jobs; backing off cutters & co. and at the end of three weeks my spirit was broken and I was on the point of resigning my post.

This was partly because the work was far more difficult than any I had before attempted, although with Mr M's help I could have managed it easily; and more because of the general attitude of antagonism. Over and over again the foreman gave me wrong or incomplete directions and altered them in such a way as to give me hours more work. I took this to be deliberate at the time, though I believe now that it was habitual bad management. I had no tools that I needed, and it was only on Saturdays that I could get to a shop. It was out of the question to borrow anything from the men. Two shop stewards informed me on the first day that they had no objection (!) to my working there provided I received the full men's rate of pay (1/3 an hour). But after this none of the men spoke to me for a long time, and would give me no help as to where to find things. My drawer was nailed up by the men, and oil was poured over everything in it through a crack another night. Had I been satisfied that my work was good I should have been content, but I felt I had not sufficient skill to hold my own against an antagonistic foreman and determined to give up. But before I had time to take steps I heard from the Ministry of Munitions that the manager had sent a good report of me and my work. He had confidently expected to see the last of me after the first three days' work.

During the four and half months that I stayed here several girls came in as turners, one as a grinder and one factory hand was promoted to the bench. Of all these I was charge-hand, and as they had only had a technical schools course behind them, I was also instructor. For absolute independence was of course expected in the shop, and these girls had not even set in their own tools before, much less ground them, and had never been allowed to touch their own belts. They were given the oldest lathes in the shop, and it was a continual struggle to get them through their work as well as to keep them contented in spite of the men. For example after the engineers' strike in May 1917 the men would not speak to us for six weeks, and though later there were times when some of them unbent they were as undependable and capricious as children, and peace could never be reckoned on for long. At the bottom of all this was, I suppose, the fear that if women became capable of doing their work they would find themselves in the Army. Thank goodness the shop was not typical.

My own work became more varied as time went on. I fitted stripping gear to two presses, and made and fitted guards to others; more drilling jigs; repairs – broken screws and punches to be extracted, cracked pawls to be replaced; backing off reamers, counterbores, and milling cutters, & c. sectioning work from various departments, the endless and varied work that usually comes to the one engineering shop in a large factory. At first I trembled every time I went to the office for a job lest it should be something I was unable to do, and even when I had grown in skill and confidence and accepted my own jobs with interest and equanimity I was still anxious as to the jobs set to the grinder. I had never done grinding myself. Luckily she knew how to keep her own stone in order; but she had only done the simplest surface and external grinding, and I had to 'keep my end up' when she was given odd angled milling cutters to sharpen, or internal grinding such as ring gauges. But she was a clever girl and soon became fairly independent.

I was withdrawn to my great relief after nearly five months. The strain would have been unbearable for much longer. The antagonism of foremen and men, the fear of disclosure of my position among them, the dread of being unable to do my work set me, the equal dread of not being able to coach the girls through their work, keeping them contented in spite of their surroundings, finally the physically hard work, the walk night and morning and the unpalatable dinner in the middle of the day. To all this was added especially in the latter part, continual air-raids and air-raid warnings; which, though they did not worry me much, did not tend to improve things.

And besides all this I had the unsatisfactory feeling that the good done was quite disproportionate to the labour involved. The girls under me were not given a chance to do good work by reason of the antiquity of their machines, and several of them drifted away soon after I left.

Two gains there were. The first a personal one, for in very few places could I have learnt so much in so short a time; nor without the treatment I received, could I have become so independent and so self reliant in my work.

The other was in the attitude of the men, they were as I have said Bolshevists and conscientious objectors. I have seen a Red Cross collector hustled out of the shop with the argument that it was the Government's war and that Government should pay Red Cross expenses. But the shop was divided against itself (one *casus belli* being the question of intercourse with the girls) and things came to a climax a week before I left. Then two thirds of the men came over to our side, and many of them even promised to devote their weekly 'Herald' penny to the Red Cross instead. The reign of the shop stewards was at an end and they never had the same power as before. In fact so complete was their fall that two of them left not long after. In September 1917 when I left Messrs A's I was made a Woman Dilution Officer, and after a week's holiday was sent to Messrs M's aeroplane works. Here very unsatisfactory work had been done by women in the fitting shop in the past, and they had consented to my temporarily organizing and instructing. As aeroplane fitting was quite new work to me another WDO accompanied me, but the work was simple enough after what I had been doing and she was recalled after a few days.

From this time on I never had factory conditions to put up with. I was given an office, had my meals from the staff canteen, and made my own hours.

I found the ten or so girls employed at filing wiring plates, clips and other small simple parts to templates; working under a charge-hand who was given no opportunity for initiative. Several of the girls were of quite unsuitable build for filing, and I exchanged them for others from the drilling and RAF wire sections and stipulated that I should interview all new hands myself. By taking on several a week we increased to fifty by the beginning of December when I left. There was no antagonism on the part of the men, and though the girls' benches were at one side of the men's fitting shop they hardly spoke to each other. The girls were always allowed to clock out five minutes before the men, and had a separate canteen, so they mixed very little. The machine was the SE5 of which the small metal fittings are more tiresome than those of any machine I have had to do with. However by keeping a watch on all work issued to the men, it was possible to select quite enough simple work for an increased number of girls; and there was quite a number of enterprising girls

Women doping wings of an aeroplane at a works near Birmingham

willing to be taught more difficult work. By December the girls' benches were responsible for all fuselage clips, besides all parts filed to templates, a great many bending jobs, riveting, small assembly jobs, soldering, & c. and I left for a week at Manchester with the Ministry of Munitions exhibition, followed by a short time at Headquarters in London.

Of the usual work of WDOs it is sufficient to say that we visited factories with a view to seeing that there was no wastage of skilled labour – that skilled labour was sufficiently diluted with semi-skilled and un-skilled.

This was at first a comparatively easy job, but grew increasingly difficult as every month went on and as skilled men were more and more called up. One or two of the WDOs were doing shop organization work each in her own line (one was a tool setter, another a welder, but the rest were occupied with this inspection work, and all the intervals between my shops I was doing the same. It is however of no general interest and I will say no more of it).

After a month of this work at one of the provincial centres, I was recalled to London to Messrs D's where I was again to organize a women's aeroplane fitting shop. This was the most satisfactory job I carried through, partly because the management gave me all the help in their power, but also the girls were very keen to learn. There was a very able woman among them too, who was promoted to charge hand.

When I started there were ten girls, without discipline, without instruction, wasting most of their time, turning out more scrap than work, when I left at the end of the month there were forty-four girls, in a better shop with 1d an hour added to their pay, as well as shortened hours, all capable of taking on any filing to templates, riveting, bending, drilling or other simple work, and of doing it in good time. The work was SE5, RE8, DH9 and 10 & c. all sub-contracts in large quantity and just suited to girls.

Unfortunately after I left the standard of skill was not kept up, primarily from want of grip on the part of the management, though it always remained a useful shop.

I only just managed to pull this job through before retiring to the country for several weeks of sick leave, after which in May, I started in quite a new line – machine tool-fitting. One of us had been needed in this branch for some time and I was given two weeks in a machine tool firm for my education. Here I worked as a hand in the fitting shop (where women were employed) and devoted most of the time to the mastery of a scraper, which I found to be a much less adaptable tool than I had expected it to be. But I learnt to scrape lathe beds, and to bed on saddles, slides, & c. After the tool-fitting I had done the actual fitting was no trouble to me.

After the less physically strenuous work of the last few months, added to five weeks of sick leave, I found the long hours and muscular strain a very severe test of endurance in spite of good conditions and no overtime, I felt so sore all over that I hardly slept the first few nights, although I had a feather bed. I was fortunate in having an excellent landlady.

After this followed more inspection work, and further experience of machine tool-fitting in various parts of the country: and at the end of June 1918 I started on my last shop organization job. This was at Messrs T's, makers of small capstan lathes, where it was proposed to give the more straightforward of the fitting work to a shop of girls, several of the men being on the point of being called up. A new shop was built for us and we started with four new hands, to which afterwards were added two more. During the seven weeks I was there these girls made considerable progress, but though they could be relied on for rough filing, chipping, harraging, and even some marking off, they none of them really mastered a scraper while I was there. Though their work would pass muster with a surface plate, they were apt to scratch, and their finish was very un-professional, while scrolling was quite beyond them. They made themselves quite useful however, and when I visited the shop a few months later they were doing well. This was of course a very ambitious undertaking, as it is work that cannot be taught in a hurry. But they were a good set of girls ready for any amount of hard work, and eager to learn, and had not the Armistice come as soon as it did, they would have proved their worth over and over again.

During the Autumn of 1918 I hoped in vain for another job. The feeling in the air that the end must soon come was so strong that firms were not prepared to reorganize. Finally came the Armistice, and as soon after as possible we were disbanded.[18]

This direct contemporary account, can be amplified by two interesting accounts, one written in October 1975, the other in January 1976.

I was born in the village of North Tolsta in the Isle of Lewis in the Outer Hebrides and I was still very young when our country was first at war with Germany. At that time there was an urgent call for female workers for jute factories in Dundee. I, along with six others, answered that call and I worked in one of Brown's factories long enough to witness my friend from Sharbost, another village in Lewis, lose part of her hand. I never saw her again because by that time I had volunteered for munitions but I believe she lost part of her hand from the wrist . . . I was called up shortly afterwards and I worked in White and Poppe's high explosive factory in Coventry. I lived in the Government Colony in a Government Hostel in the ten-der care of Matron Crawford, No. 10 Hostel. I worked with black powder and that was called loading, and I also worked with TNT and tetryl. I was transferred to another high explosives factory in Birmingham and I was there when the war came to an end . . .

I wasn't quite 17 years of age when I first went to Coventry and money did not mean a thing to us in those days. I know I had no money sense anyway, it was just a question of helping our country in the best way we knew how. We were a happy bunch and we made our own fun. I shall never forget the first day on the press in Coventry. I know I was trembling watching the hands of a big clock make their way up to one thousand. I had my two hands on two levers when two warm gentle hands covered mine and guided them till the hands of the clock touched one thousand. My confidence was complete after that. The two hands belonged to a ranking military gentleman in hospital blue uniform.[19]

The second account reads:

I was in domestic service and 'hated every minute of it' when war broke out, earning £2 a month working from 6.00 a.m. to 9.00 p.m. So when the need came for women 'war workers' my chance came to 'out'.

I started on hand cutting shell fuses at the converted war works at the ACs Thames Ditton, Surrey. It entailed the finishing off by 'hand dies' the machine cut thread on the fuses that held the powder for the big shells, so had to be very accurate so that the cap fitted perfectly. We worked twelve hours a day apart from the journey morning and night at Kingston-upon-Thames. Believe me we were very ready for bed in those days, and as for wages I thought I was very well off earning £5 a week. While at the ACs I remember a 'zeppelin' got as far as London. We all had to go below ground in an old wood store. (We were more afraid of the rats, big water ones, the works being alongside the river Thames near Hampton Court, than the zeppelin.)

I left the ACs in 1916 for a much cleaner and lighter job at the 'Wireless' Teddington where they made the wireless boxes for the signallers in the communications lines in France. They were some of the first such instruments of wireless to be used in warfare, and no doubt the same as my husband was using as he gained his MM [Military Medal] mending the communication lines under heavy shellfire as a Volunteer.[20]

Working in a Munitions factory could be physically extremely unpleasant and could carry risks to health; it could also be downright dangerous. Two women Medical Officers in the Munitions factories, both of whom had degrees from Edinburgh University which had been giving women full medical degrees for many years, wrote a painstaking report on the effects of TNT on women workers for *Lancet* of 12 August 1916. It described the irritative symptoms which women developed: throat and/or chest tight, sore, swollen and burning; coughing, sometimes a thick yellow phlegm with bitter taste; pain around waist and in abdomen; nausea, vomiting, constipation at first, then diarrhoea; rashes and eruptions on skin. These could in turn lead to toxic symptoms: digestive, as in the irritative stage in jaundice; circulatory, giddiness, hot and cold flushes, swelling, etc.; cerebral, drowsiness, loss of memory, disorders of sight; delirium, coma, and convulsions. Doctors Agnes Livingstone-Fairmont and Barbara Martin-Cunningham recommended that all women recruited for work on TNT should be very carefully selected with regard to their physical characteristics. None should be under 21 nor over 40. Factories should be adequately ventilated, and the women should be provided with good and protective clothing. They should only work for short periods on TNT and be taken off regularly for other types of work.

Women working on TNT, then, could often be quite seriously ill; yet they were sometimes jocularly referred to as 'canaries' because of the discoloration of the skin brought about by the symptoms of TNT poisoning. The same issue of *Lancet* that published the careful medical report, contained an all too typical, unfeeling, bombastic, and not to say male chauvinist leading article: 'It is so often the case that it is the neglect, on the part of the worker, to follow such simple precautions which leads to a disturbance of health. They are offered authoritative help, but refuse to help themselves; and the observance of such regulations can be made with little inconvenience and be still consistent with a maximum output of munitions.'

The biggest single concentration of women workers was at the new national cordite factory at Gretna. There 11,000 women were employed, most of them housed in specially built hostels at Gretna, East Riggs, and

Carlisle. Out of every hundred women at Gretna, 36 had formerly been in domestic service, 20 had lived at home, 15 had already worked in another munitions factory, 12 had worked in ordinary factories, 5 had been shop assistants, and 12 had been laundry workers, farm hands, dressmakers, school teachers, or clerks. The need to produce the highest possible output, went hand in hand with Victorian ideas: 'With the object of keeping the workers within the Factory area, and away from undesirable temptations elsewhere, no late ordinary evening trains were run between Gretna and Carlisle except on Saturdays, when the latest train left the neighbouring City at 9.30 p.m.'[21] However, the officials running the complex were sensitive enough to see the need to secure additional Treasury funds to provide recreational facilities. A two-storey institute was built at Gretna, the ground floor for men, the upper for women. The men's floor was 'plentifully supplied with monthly magazines, weekly illustrated journals, and daily newspapers; and cards, draughts, dominoes, chess and other games are provided'. The distinctions felt to be appropriate to the different leisure patterns of the two sexes are apparent: 'The girls have a most comfortable Reading and Writing Room with magazines, newspapers, and a library at their disposal; a dainty Lounge supplied with several sewing machines; a Games Room that possesses a piano and a very large gramophone'.

These facilities were free, but women wishing to attend the weekly 'socials' held on Wednesday had to pay a club subscription. They could then bring their men friends. A subscription also had to be paid for membership of the Mixed Club which met two or three nights a week. A great deal of football was played at the Gretna hostels, 'though the number of Leagues steadily diminished as more and more men were called away from the Munitions factories to serve in the trenches. There were one or two football clubs for girls, a good many of whom played the game really well; but there had been some division of opinion as to the wisdom of encouraging them to pursue this branch of sport. They have not been prohibited from doing so, and some pitches have been made available for them of which good use is made.' It was, however, without reserve felt to be perfectly appropriate for women to play hockey.[22]

The most serious disaster at Gretna took place early in 1917 when a large building containing several tons of nitro-glycerine suddenly disappeared in a lightning sheet of flame, with a crash that could be heard far into the countryside. One girl was killed, and many were injured by flying debris and glass. The girls were commended for the coolness with which they acted in the crisis.

There was a much more serious explosion at Silvertown in East London in which a dozen women were killed; and there were a number of other incidents throughout the country resulting in well over 200 deaths.

Woman suffragists in the Manchester area established in May 1915 a Women's War Interests Committee chiefly to monitor women's conditions in the munitions factories. The Committee reckoned that the best remedy was trade union organization, but by January 1916 less than 12 per cent of the female munitions workers in the district belonged to unions: the National Union of Railwaymen and Amalgamated Association of Tramway and Vehicle Workers were now open to women, but the Amalgamated Society of Engineers, by the letter of its constitution remained closed to women. Prejudice was apparent in the Tramway Workers' resolution of May 1915 that the employment of women on the tramways was a dangerous and unwise innovation. The Manchester and Salford Trades and Labour Council in July passed a resolution that no

RIGHT Women railway
workers cleaning carriages
BELOW Women brewery
workers in Cheshire
washing casks

ABOVE Women road sweepers
working in the Borough of
Ealing in London
LEFT Post woman collecting
mail from a pillar box

women should be employed while it was possible to obtain men; and when
in August, Salford Corporation engaged women to work on the tramways
a number of men refused to work with them.

However by the autumn a central change in male trade union thinking
is apparent: the attempt to exclude women has changed to an insistence
that women be paid the same rates as men. The development of this new
male attitude is once again crucial to developing full *female* emancipation
By the end of the year half the Manchester tram conductors were women
there were several drivers in other parts of Lancashire. Sometimes women
did not turn round the trolley, which could be a reason for denying them
war bonuses paid instead to the male driver who undertook this extra
task. Resistance continued to the employment of women in those branches
of the cotton industry hitherto reserved for men: the mule-spinning
rooms and dyeing, bleaching and finishing. The Committee expressed
some sympathy for the idea that conditions in these branches were too
arduous and unpleasant for women. Even after a trade union agreement

Woman dentist
examining teeth

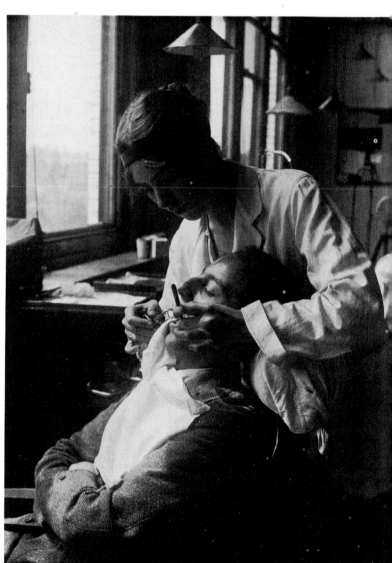

admitting women had been signed, women showed no enthusiasm for entering the Oldham spinning rooms. Here we do see women's physical constitution as a possible barrier to equality. Echoing the confessions of exhaustion given in the long account quoted at the beginning of this section, the Committee declared: 'Engineering work for women is heavy and exhausting and it is doubtful whether night work does not put too heavy a strain on the nervous system of the average woman worker.'[23]

Conscription and its Consequences

The voluntary registration scheme for women of March 1915 was designed more for show than for effect. However, by the summer the manpower shortage, and in particular the insatiable demands of the trenches, had become so serious that the Government decided to compile a compulsory National Register. On Sunday 15 August, all persons, female as well as male, between the ages of 15 and 65 had to register, rather as they did at the time of the decennial census, particulars of age and occupation. It was still Military Service for men, rather than national service for women, which was the main preoccupation. In November, Lord Derby's famous scheme, using all the resources of Government and moral pressure short of outright conscription, was brought into force: men were called upon to 'attest' that they would serve if and when required. The Derby scheme did not produce the men required, but it did produce the right tactical background against which on 5 January 1916 Asquith could introduce the first Military Service Bill providing for conscription of all single men. But even this was not enough. After a stormy secret session on 25 April, the Universal Conscription Bill was introduced at the beginning of May. While these plans for the military conscription of men were being matured a parallel initiative in regard to the civil employment of women was taken in November 1915 when the Home Secretary and the President of the Board of Trade established the Women's Employment Committee.

The imposition of Universal Conscription was an event of central importance in the social history of the war: it began the second and definitive growth in women's employment and determined that the changes involved should go far beyond a limited expansion and upgrading of industrial labour, given additional piquancy by the entry for the first time into hard physical work of a few adventurous members of the upper classes. Just two weeks after the passing of the Act, the Government launched its first national drive to fill the places vacated or about to be vacated by men. Only now did the wartime pattern of women's employment begin to assume its final shape. When, in early 1917, an official National Service Scheme was introduced to cover all aspects of civilian and non-combatant employment, it was concerned as much with women as with men.

In July 1914 there had been 212,000 women employed in the various metal and engineering industries that were to become the ones most directly connected with war production. The figure for July 1915, 256,000, shows only a relatively small increase; but the greater expansion of later 1915, combined with the impact of conscription, is seen in the next July figure, 520,000, an increase of over 100 per cent. There was still a great deal of slack, so that by July 1917 when the National Service Scheme had had six months to take effect the figure was 819,000; in the last year of the war there was a further increase of well over 100,000.

In industry as a whole the total employment of women and girls over 10 had increased between 1914 and 1918 by about 800,000, from 2,179,000 to 2,971,000.

On the whole, before conscription, accounts of women taking over men's work tended to be exaggerated: society, like a pub packed full of men, was from the start overconscious of any feminine intrusion. The press, in any case, was starved by the censorship of most hard news, and found that the many articles on the new roles of women were very popular while also serving the patriotic purpose encouraging women to seek useful employment. The odd encounter with a woman ticket collector or conductress might seem to suggest a massive female takeover when in fact only a few outposts had been established. Actually, the London General Omnibus Company was not converted to the use of women conductresses till February 1916; in March there were still only 100 bus conductresses in London, though training schemes were by then on hand to provide another 500 women a month.

Beneath the flamboyant froth of exaggerated press accounts, the hard reality was of continuing male prejudice against the employment of women wherever this could be avoided, and of a corresponding resentment among women that their desire to serve was being spurned. In July 1916 *Women's Industrial News* commented sharply on popular misconceptions as to the employment of women in agriculture: 'Most of the press paragraphs referring to the replacement of men by women upon farms have been calculated to give an erroneous impression to the unknowing public. The demand for female labour in agriculture during 1915 was not very great and large numbers of girls who offered to take up such work failed to find employment.' A couple of months later the agricultural organizing officer at Worcester Labour Exchange was begging the Board of Agriculture to stop giving exemptions from military service to farm labourers since 'the farmers in spite of everything we have tried to say or do will not take a woman if they can get anything in the shape of a man.'[24]

By February 1917 the total number of bus conductresses had jumped up from the select few of the previous year to around two and a half thousand, some half of whom, it was said, were former domestic servants. Over the whole war it is transport that shows the biggest proportionate increase in women's employment – from 18,000 in 1914 to 117,000 in 1918. After transport, the biggest proportional increases were in clerical, commercial, administrative and educational activities. In banking and finance there was a fantastic rate of growth – from a mere 9,500 female employees in 1914 to 63,700 in 1917. Taking the entire span of the war, the number of women and girls employed in the role of commerce and its allied occupations grows from 505,000 to 934,000. In National and Local Government, in which education is included, numbers rose from 262,000 to 460,000. It is in these arid statistics that we encounter a central phenomenon in the sociology of women's employment in the twentieth century, the rise of the business girl, taking the term to cover the whole range from executive secretary to shorthand-typist. The growth of large scale industry and bureaucracy would undoubtedly have brought this development eventually, but it was the war which, in creating simultaneously a proliferation of Government committees and departments and a shortage of men, brought a sudden and irreversible advance in the economic and social power of a category of women employees which extended from sprigs of the aristocracy to daughters of the proletariat. 'No woman worker is greater in demand than the shorthand-typist,' stated the *Daily Mail* in September 1915, adding that wages had in a year risen from £1 to 35s per week.

A woman tram conductress could sometimes receive cooperation, sometimes hostility, from her male fellow workers; but she often enjoyed

pecially favourable attention from her public. One former tram conductress in Lancashire recalls that she 'was one of the ladies who were
asked to learn to drive the trams'. She was ready to take over, 'when the
men drivers objected', reinforcing their point with a strike. Instead, she
was made an inspector. 'Some of the drivers were very annoyed. I would
get on a tram and the driver would put the brake on and send me flying to
the top of the tram. Some of the men passengers would not show their
tickets. Some of the men conductors would not hand over their book to
check. But I managed.' Because of wartime restrictions business men and
professional people made use of the trams. This particular conductress
obviously welcomed the special attentions they gave her, and remembers
that one shipping broker 'brought a rose from his garden for me to wear
off duty'.[25]

Men had been driving tramcars back into the previous century; hence
their resistance to any intrusion by women was strongest. Traditionally
there had always been some acceptance of the idea of there being a kind of
affinity between women and horses. From early in the war, small numbers
of girls and women were employed increasingly in stables, and on
veterinary work. From late 1915 on, and more markedly after the introduction of conscription, they took over as van drivers of horse drawn vehicles
without much opposition. The driving of motor vehicles was scarcely a
well-established tradition yet, and here the emergence of women drivers
seems to have taken place with little opposition. Many upper-class
women already knew how to drive a car; there were many advertisements
from garages offering training in this skill to women. The Metropolitan
Asylums Board Motor Ambulance Section was the first major public
body to employ women drivers, this from the beginning of 1916. By July
1916 the London County Council Ambulance Corps was run entirely by
women. Its main function was to deal with street accidents. There is a
fascinating account written up in 1921 by a journalist, Dorothy Longmuir,
of her work with the Metropolitan Asylums Board. Towards the end of
1915 Miss Longmuir saw one of the Board's advertisements for women
competent to drive. Despite its title, the Board's work in this respect
mainly consisted of taking the infectious sick from their homes to hospitals. The need was already urgent because all the male drivers had
attested under the Derby scheme (and perceptive employers, therefore,
could see that conscription was imminent). Miss Longmuir was given a
driving test, a medical test, and then became the first woman ambulance
driver based at the North West station, Lawn Road, Hampstead. She was
given a 20–25 h.p. Siddeley-Deasy 4 cylinder ambulance to drive, from
garages which had really been designed for horse transport. Here is her
account:

> These cars were not fitted with windscreens and as the Board
> expected us to wear uniform caps like the men (really a sort of
> railway porter's cap) the absence of a screen made things a little
> difficult, I mean in the way of keeping the cap on . . .
> We were, we understood through the Board, the first organized
> body of women employed in England for such work and the uniform
> question was rather acute for some time.
> Before we began work, blue serge Norfolk jackets and skirts (stock
> sizes) had been ordered. Of course we were none of us stock size and
> the process of fitting caused a lot of amusement. Ultimately, these
> garments were satisfactorily made to measure. Footgear we provided
> ourselves, but gaiters were part of the official uniform. The first

suggestion was a stiff leather gaiter as worn by men with a vertical spring – this we found quite impossible. Next we had a contraption of loose American cloth, like spats at the bottom with circular springs to go round the ankle and calf. These were ineffably clumsy and ineffective, and attracted the attention of the children in the streets who took us for men, more or less badly disguised as women. The gaiters were also horribly uncomfortable to wear, and we were very glad to be able to persuade the Board to give us ordinary soft leather buttoned gaiters.

The cap question was temporarily solved by the provision of a soft mackintosh cap quite shapeless and hot to wear. After many protests we eventually got a VAD pattern cap with a light blue band to distinguish us from the members of that body.

At first serge overcoats were issued to us, too light but not waterproof. Afterwards we had a splendid Melton cloth coat which gave the most ample protection. We also had oilskins . . .

Miss Longmuir found the Siddeley-Deasy easy to handle. It was not till 1917 that the Board purchased a number of Talbots. 'These were much more beautiful in our eyes than the Siddeley-Deasys although we relinquished the latter with some regret. The Talbots had windscreens and were comfortable and easy to drive in spite of their power, which was almost too high for driving in traffic.' She continues:

One duty we did not altogether appreciate was the night washing of cars . . .

We also had to wash down the yard, a tremendous job on account of the oil and grease which, in patches, we found very adhesive, but as we were assured that the men had always done it, we tackled it wholeheartedly . . .

The part of our cleaning work we really enjoyed was polishing up the engines. This we did *con amore*, and the more speckless our engines were the more we loved them. Old silk blouses made good polishers for copper work . . .

Daily intercourse with so many different types inevitably modified our own individuality and to use a common phrase rubbed many corners off . . .

Even our cubicles were not the private bedrooms we had been used to, and it was amusing to hear the conversations (sometimes rather personal) which were carried on from one to the other . . .

Often 12 to 13 hours a day were worked, but, most hard to bear, often with long periods in which there was nothing to do. From time to time, the girls also drove buses full of convalescing patients. To begin with the North West Station was the only one staffed with women, but then Dorothy Longmuir transferred, first to the Brook Station near the Royal Arsenal and then to Fulham: by the end of the war the Board was employing over 50 women drivers.

. . . On the whole our life was an extremely happy one, but in some respects, of course, difficult at first, due to the strangeness of the work . . .

Our worst experiences were night journeys made during the years of reduced lighting. Our own cars had no lights worth speaking of, and the task of driving in unfamiliar streets was sometimes difficult. At the Brook Station we had a good deal of fog in winter and on a

OPPOSITE Police constable directing London woman ambulance driver to the scene of an accident

foggy night, we often had to cross Blackheath at a snail's pace, one of us walking ahead to keep in touch with the side of the road.

London ambulance woman giving first aid to a child injured in a street accident

Nevertheless, Miss Longmuir was very proud to note that the women ambulance drivers had remarkably few accidents. When called upon to volunteer for air-raid duty, all the girls did so, though work during air-raids was 'very trying to our nerves'. Noting that 'we were throughout expected to do all the duties the men had done and we were paid the same rate as the men,' Miss Longmuir concluded, 'I look back on these years as among my happiest.'

Driving motor vehicles tended to be an occupation of upper-class women. The enormous range of other activities open to women from 1916 onwards was undertaken by women of all social classes. One former draper's assistant, whose father was a railway porter, also worked as a porter in the Glasgow Central Station parcels office during the war; she went back to the draper's shop at the end of the war, but already early in 1918 her work had brought a meeting with her future husband (one personal aspect of many women's wartime experiences that we find repeated again and again).[26]

Women worked as lamplighters and as window cleaners. They also did very heavy work in gasworks and foundries, carrying bags of coke and working among the furnaces. We have a pleasant reminiscence of one of the simple remedies used when the women succumbed to the arduous nditions under which they were working: 'Many is the time the girls ould be affected by the gas, the remedy being to walk them up and down in e fresh air, and then drink a bottle of guiness.'[27]

Despite repeated, though perhaps rather spongy, government-initiated tempts to recruit women workers for the land, these had not been nspicuously successful. In July 1915 there were about 20,000 less ermanent female workers on the land than in July 1914 – as in the case of omestic service the war had provided a blessed release. The deficiency as not made good by the 8,000 additional casual female workers on the nd. By July 1916 permanent female workers in England and Wales were p 22,000 on 1914, but in Scotland the drain (and the temptations of better-aid employment) was irresistible and employment was down 2,000. On e land the feudal tradition was specially strong, and there was a heavy mphasis on trying to secure recruits from the more respectable classes society. For example, the joint Board of Trade and Board of Agriculture aflet, *War Agricultural Service for Women* of 1915, remarked:

If, for instance, women and girls of high standing socially, who live in a dairying district, will at once learn to milk, and will let the other inhabitants see them going, in suitable working-dress, to and from their work day after day – then their social inferiors will not be slow to follow their example, and employers of labour will take them seriously.

Lady Londonderry pushed enthusiastically ahead with organizing omen's land work through the Women's Legion totally independently of e Women's Department of the Board of Trade. Two rather different ivil Service reactions were minuted on the same day, 3 March 1916. The

Members of the Women's Forage Department feeding a hay baler. Note the long dresses. Compare pages 123 and 124

first reads: 'We can't prevent Lady Londonderry expanding her organization wherever she likes and if she gets ahead of the Board of Trade and gets the work done we need not complain.' The second reads: 'I agree that it would be unfortunate if Lady Londonderry did not work in cooperation with the Board of Trade.' In the upshot, aristocratic connections prevailed, and the Women's Legion was given a Board of Trade grant of several hundred pounds. As late as September 1916, the Permanent Secretary at the Board of Agriculture was minuting: 'It is all very well for, say, the local duchess to be brought into a new movement at its inception, mainly because her name is of value in an advertisement and because her purse is useful to provide the necessary funds, but when the movement has once been started, unless the duchess has the good sense to efface herself as quickly as possible and allow the project to be carried on by the people who are primarily interested in it, in nine times out of ten the scheme is bound to fail.'

The first 'Demonstrations' – that is to say competitions in farming skill – exclusively for women were held at Launceston in Cornwall on 9 March 1916. Others followed. Of a 'Demonstration' held at Biddenham in June 1916 it was reported that 'most of the onlookers were women of the right class', and that 'the entrants were apparently daughters of farmers or villagers of good class'.[28] In January 1916 another voluntary organization was launched, the Women's National Land Service Corps, 'a mobile force of educated women to help in recruiting and organizing the local labour of women'.[29]

The idea of women police, which the National Union of Women Workers and other organizations had urged before the war, got its first real impetus from the first dislocations of war, and, in particular, from the sudden appearance of vast new military training camps, and the transportation across the country of bodies of soldiers. In July 1915, largely through the good offices of Lloyd George, the Women's Police Service entered into a contractual arrangement with the Ministry of Munitions whereby it was to supply women police for service at munitions factories where large numbers of women were employed. In 1916 a special Act of Parliament, relating to factories, made it possible for the salaries of full-time police women to be chargeable to the police fund. Of the 1,080 women trained and equipped by the WPS, 985 were allocated to munitions factories. Meantime the women police patrols continued to develop their work which was mainly concentrated in the cities and around the big military camps.

The familiar upper-class tone comes through in a letter written by Miss Goldingham of the WPS to Mrs Charles Furse, Commandant in Chief of the women's VADs, on 23rd February 1916, explaining the work of the WPS: 'We get this training free and are glad to welcome recruits who may wish to take up the work in either a voluntary or a professional capacity. Authorities are of the opinion that educated gentlewomen should be appointed to the professional posts now being opened in the provinces.'[30] In fact, as can be seen from Appendix 5, getting on for half of the total number of WPS recruits were of private means or of no profession; only a fifth at the most came from working-class occupations.

Apart from their work at and around the munitions factories – the women police at Gretna station, for instance, had to be sure that women workers travelling to the Gretna factory went in the 'Ladies only' compartments which made up the bulk of the train – the Women's Police Service listed its activities as: patrolling, attendance at police courts, domiciliary visiting, and supervision of Music Halls, cinemas, etc. The

Women coke workers lifting a bag on to a woman carrier's back

big railway stations were constantly patrolled and, the WPS claimed, the authorities frequently expressed their thanks for the valuable assistance given at the time of arrival or departure of troop trains. Parks, public grounds, unfrequented roads, railway bridges, etc. were patrolled by policewomen; they regularly watched crossings when the schools emptied, also canal and river banks, 'which are great sources of danger to small children'. It was claimed too that the WPS were able to check roughness and quarrelling and to prevent boys from gambling, destroying property, and throwing stones, and also that 'in notoriously troublesome districts the mere presence of policewomen in uniform seems to exercise a beneficial influence and they have been very successful in dealing with brawls and street fights'.

It was one of the duties of the policewomen regularly to attend the police court in their district and to be present during the hearing of cases dealing with women and children. Magistrates came to make frequent use of the services of policewomen to investigate cases which did not come under the police missionaries or probation officers. 'It is of the utmost benefit to women in cases of assault,' the WPS very rightly said, 'that the investigation should be conducted by women and not by men.' The domiciliary visiting aspect of women police work was very much the sort of thing that would now be done by professional social workers. In a sense one can see here women being employed in what could be regarded as specifically women's work not really analogous to normal police duties. Indeed, as the WPS report itself said, domiciliary visiting had 'been advocated by several Chief Constables as being more particularly work for women than for men'.[31] Supervision in cinemas, we shall return to when we consider manners, morals, and leisure activities.

The Women Patrols advanced slowly from being a kind of moral protection service to an almost fully accepted arm of the normal police force in certain towns. The limitations on the part of the patrols in 1915 as well as prevailing moral attitudes, are apparent in an internal report of August 1915: 'Here we have several open grass patches which are very dangerous, as young couples lie there in the dark, and even in daylight such things are seen that we have been obliged to call the attention of the police, as it was outside our duties to interfere. I am glad to say I have seen the police on several occasions removing such couples, as it is such an easy thing for young girls to copy things they see around them. As a rule, however, they behave better when they see the Patrols.' It was admitted that the Patrols were often at first thought of as 'interfering toads', but, the organizers of the Patrols congratulated themselves, after a while mothers began to think it rather wonderful that these women should 'leave their homes and go about so quiet and ladylike'.[32]

Apart from the uniform, the women, of course, had their identity cards. But at Reading, the Chief Constable insisted on adding to the cards a formally printed statement: 'I, the undersigned, am in no way responsible for the conduct of this Patrol.' However, the Chief Constable really did have to eat his words, for in May 1917 Reading appointed two policewomen because of 'the excellent work done by the women patrols'. There was no recantation by the Manchester Chief Constable who throughout the war refused to recognize women patrols or sign their authorization cards, and of course the women did meet many resistances. Liverpool showed itself in advance of Manchester, when in April 1917 ten women police were appointed along with the first woman police sergeant. Altogether by the end of the war 29 towns and one county were employing women police or women patrols.[33]

WOMEN IN UNIFORM

Autumn 1916–November 1918

The Turning of the Screw

In the autumn of 1916 increasing pressure was put on the Asquith Coalition Government to take a firmer grip on the war effort. The ousting of Asquith, and the establishment of the Lloyd George Coalition Government in December 1916, marked a definitive stage towards direct State control of all aspects of the war effort in place of the mixture of Government and voluntary action which had characterized the earlier part of the war. Domestic life itself took on the grim hue of uniformity, and there was much evidence of privation and war weariness. Whereas to begin with the various uniformed women's organizations had in large measure been the pet projects of a number of strong-willed individual women, the Government now began a systematic organization of the women's auxiliary military services.

The idea of traditional 'peasant' costume, which stressed femininity, for women in certain occupations, for example flower sellers, or Scottish fishwives, went back for centuries. Lancashire working women had their shawls and clogs, and many overworked housewives could be said to be wearing their own special uniform, a drab black. But uniform, in the traditional masculine sense, associated with military and police organizations, was unknown to all but a tiny handful of individualists among British women till the nineteenth century. First of all there were the girls' Public Schools, modelled on the famous boys' Public Schools. Then in the Edwardian period came the founding of the Girl Guides' Movement. Nurses, from the time when Florence Nightingale put the profession on a respectable basis, had had their 'distinctive' uniform, but it did not suppress femininity. With the launching of the FANYS and the VADs before the First World War another slight step was taken towards para-military uniform.

It was sometimes assumed by men that if women did take on positions of authority they would never manage to cooperate with each other but would behave with all the cattiness of the stereotyped male image of women. Certainly it did become clear that such tough and autocratic ladies as Dame Katherine Furse, Commandant of the Women's VADs, and Lady Londonderry, founder of the Women's Legion, could be as determined to stand on their dignity as any man.

Because the conditions of trench warfare were so horrific, with infantrymen pitted again and again against high explosives and machine gun fire, the rate of mutilation and serious injury was far higher than anyone had expected, leading very quickly to a dire shortage at the Front of trained nurses. The Women's VAD organization laboured under several difficulties. It was under the management of the British Red Cross Society and the Order of St John of Jerusalem, both supposed to be international bodies concerned purely with works of mercy, something of an anomaly in this most bitter of national wars. The central joint VA Committee, representing the three parent bodies, was chaired by a dull aristocrat, Sir Arthur Stanley, and the Committee was composed entirely of men.

The Volunteer Aid Detachments, as the title makes clear, were voluntary organizations with no resources to pay their workers; they were scarcely equipped for service overseas though a handful of adventurous girls from upper-class backgrounds did go to France in 1914. Then in 1915, to try to meet the shortage of nurses, the military authorities introduced direct payment at the rate of £20 per annum eventually rising to a maximum of £30 per annum for nurses working in military hospitals. However, such payment by the War Office conflicted with the status of the VADs under the Red Cross; thus the War Office was tempted to turn to the Women's Legion: specially selected members were employed as nurses and to the chagrin of Lady Londonderry fitted out in the standard VAD nursing uniform. There was therefore a triangle of friction between Mrs Furse, Lady Londonderry and Sir Arthur Stanley's Central Committee which remained exclusively male till well on into 1916.

By September 1916 there were 8,000 VADs serving in military hospitals. The careful selection procedure and use of references made clear that these women were, and were intended to be, very middle class or upper class in background. Most of them were working under the new 'General Service' scheme initiated in June 1916, whereby direct payment was made by the military authorities, and whereby VADs undertook cooking, clerical work, dispensing, storekeeping, and so on, as well as nursing.

Mrs Furse was genuinely torn between the desire to protect her members, whose goodwill was often shamelessly exploited, and her traditional *noblesse oblige* sentiments, and clearsighted recognition that however uncongenial the conditions under which VADs laboured, this was nothing compared with what serving men were going through. On one occasion she wrote 'I must confess I hope that women will be content to accept such rates as they can afford to accept. Ours are "cushy" jobs compared with what the men have gone to.' She added that four women were doing the work of three men, whereas eight women took up the accommodation of fourteen to twenty-five men. Furthermore, 'women have spring bedsteads where men sleep on boards', and 'women have special rations including milk, where the man does without milk'.[34] Hostility from the nursing profession, particularly the senior grades, was no doubt understandable, but it did not make the lot of the VAD any easier to bear. Katherine Furse accumulated a file on 'intolerance on part of Sister and trained nurses'. A couple of examples give the flavour:

> . . . having done no nursing or hospital work before was put into a very heavy surgical ward and made to help with terribly bad dressings and even given eye dressings to do herself with no help or instruction from the Sister. She was so upset by the awful sights and the fear of making mistakes that her nerves were upset and she either had bad nightmares about her work or could not sleep at all. The Matron transferred her to a Medical Ward but would not promise to keep her there and so she felt she had better leave. She was interviewed by Mrs Cane 1.10.16 who said the girl had evidently suffered a great strain and had lost about a stone during the month in hospital. Mrs Cane knew her personally and considered under the right conditions she would probably have made an admirable nurse.

Another case: At Beaufort War Hospital. She was told by her Charge Sister 'that she was usurping the professional's place' and under such circumstances it did not seem proper to her remain . . .[35]

With all the stresses and strains, rivalries with other women, and hostility from men, Mrs Furse was clear by September 1916 what the answer ought to be: 'Personally I have been convinced the last 6 months that if the war continues we shall require some form of Conscription or Enlistment to supply sufficient suitable women for the needs of the Government in various spheres of work.'[36] Mrs Furse herself drew up a number of draft schemes for a women's military auxiliary corps with, of course, all the inevitable emphasis on problems of discipline, morality, and enlisting women of the right social class. While she was doing this the Woman's Land Service Corps was itself (December 1916) putting forward a scheme for a Land Army on military lines. The Government too, now under Lloyd George, was beginning to stir into action.

The WAAC

The story of the WAAC is a perfect paradigm of the prejudices, preconceptions, and preoccupations which rise to the surface when there is any question of integrating women into some particular aspect of a man's world. On 8 December 1916 the War Office instructed Lieutenant-General

Women's Army Auxiliary Corps Recruiting Sergeant enrolling recruits in Trafalgar Square, London

H. M. Lawson to report on the number and physical categories of men employed out of the fighting area in France. General Lawson's report of 16 January 1917 recommended employing women in the army in France, and in support of this he cited the example of what was already happening on the domestic front. A series of discussions on the enlistment of women in the army had already begun, and the various interests and prejudices were only too apparent. The Adjutant-General, Sir Neville Macready, was most anxious that women could be treated exactly as soldiers in order to make sure that there was no trade union influence over them.[37] Lord Derby, the War Secretary, was broadly in agreement but was anxious 'not to give outside associations of women an opportunity for agitation'.[38] He preferred to bring in selected Uncle Toms (or perhaps one should say Auntie Toms). In fact, the leading women knew what was going on and Katherine Furse addressed two letters to Sir Reginald Grade at the War Office expressing the fear that proper consultation with women was being ignored:

> The dilution of the Army by women can only be successfully carried out if the whole Mother wit of women can be brought to bear on it.

Mrs Fawcett and other women's leaders addressed a letter on the same point to Lloyd George.[39]

At the end of January Mrs Chalmers Watson, a distinguished medical woman in Edinburgh and sister of the Director General of National Service, Sir Auckland Geddes, was summoned to attend a meeting in London convened by Lord Derby. Mrs Chalmers Watson was shown the Lawson report and given permission to discuss it with a number of other women. Evidence for what went on in these discussions is contained both in the rather bare formal minutes and in notes of two interviews which Mrs Chalmers Watson gave in June 1918.[40] Lord Derby was against the full enlistment of women though he was aware that if any women were captured they might then be treated by the Germans as civilians dressed up (a problem which was never solved in the First World War, and which never in fact came up). Other matters discussed concerned discipline, and the manner in which women should be remunerated. The meeting broke up inconclusively, and Mrs Chalmers Watson was recommended by her brother to seek a personal interview with Sir Neville Macready. According to her account:

> On this occasion he was very friendly and asked her opinion of all women at the Meeting. They discussed them for one and a half hours. Mrs Chalmers Watson said they were of two types; the anti-suffrage woman who believed in getting her way by cajolery and the suffrage type of professional worker. Sir Neville Macready said he preferred the professional women and asked her for her ideas as to how this scheme could be worked. She had made out rough notes with Miss Anderson about this and he kept them, and said he wished to meet her again on Friday 14 February.
>
> On the Friday he asked her if she would head this scheme if Lord Derby approved. He said 'Lord Derby wishes a lady of title. I want a working woman'.

Mrs Chalmers Watson said she wanted time to think things over, and meantime went on a tour of inspection in France, which in turn led to a kind of *de facto* assumption on her part of the position of Chief Controller of the new organization. The Commander-in-Chief in the field, General Sir Douglas Haig, conveyed his view to the War Office on 11 March 1917

Women's Army Auxiliary Corps marching in Rouen, 24 July 1917

that 'the principle of employing women in this Country [i.e. France] is accepted and they will be made use of wherever conditions admit'. He then, however, appended a long list of 'objections and difficulties'. 'It is necessary to point out,' said Sir Douglas, 'that there is a limit with regard to the extent to which replacement by unfit men, women and coloured labour can be carried out with safety, and this limit can only be decided in this Country.' With regard to bakery work he argued that as 'women cannot be employed with the troops, provision will have to be made for detaching a Field Bakery when necessary to supply a detached body of troops'. It would be possible for hospitals to take women cooks, but men would be necessary for such tasks as lifting carcasses of beef. 'Clothing storekeepers cannot be women, for they cannot assist at the trying on of clothes.'[41] But whatever reservations Sir Douglas Haig might have the wheels were already turning.

Selection Boards were set up and recruitment was carried on through the office of the Director General of National Service. Applicants had to have two references, and apart from the Selection Board, had to go before a Medical Board on which all the doctors were women. Before the end of the month more women had applied than there were places for. Yet the first Army Council instruction recognizing that 'the employment of women at the Base and on the Lines of Communications abroad has been approved' did not appear till 28 March, and the famous Army Council instruction No. 1069 of 1917 which is the formal basis of the WAAC under that title, did not appear until 7 July 1917. The delays were caused by a continued shuffling within the War Office over where control of the women should actually lie. Colonel Leigh Wood hoped to become himself Chief Controller of the WAAC with Mrs Chalmers Watson being designated Chief Woman Controller. However, in the upshot Mrs Chalmers Watson was Chief Controller, with a staff of controllers and administrators, general control, nevertheless, being vested in the Adjutant-General's Department. In May it was decided that there should be recruitment to the WAAC for service at home as well as in France, and the perennial discussion of discipline, uniforms, hours of work and methods of payment continued. On discipline, General Charles Buckley stated that any question of detention or field punishment would be 'ridiculous', the former, in particular, 'and I have no intention to accept lady inmates in my detention barracks'.

WAAC cooks working in the camp kitchen at Abbéville, 15 September 1917

One rooted, immemorial tradition was that a commission from the Crown could go to male subjects only. Thus there were no military ranks

AC cooks in an infantry
np preparing vegetables,
ux, 24 July 1917

in the WAAC. Instead of officers, there were controllers and administrators, and instead of NCOs, there were forewomen. In her own draft plan, Mrs Furse had insisted that 'enough stress cannot be made on the fact that the women should, as far as possible, be drawn from the upper middle and middle classes'. In fact, many 'lower-class' women enrolled for the rank and file. All administrators were to start at the lowest rate of £120 per annum: the highest possible rate was £500 per annum, but very few ever got over £250 per annum. The other ranks were to be paid in accordance with the category of work undertaken. The minimum for unskilled work was to be 24/- per week, while expert shorthand-typists could earn 45/- per week. There was a 12/6 per week deduction for rations: uniform and quarters were free. Members of the WAAC working in Britain, could, if this did not interfere with their efficiency, live at home: such women, however, were not to be employed as cooks – the fear was, quite crudely, that they would steal the food supplies and take them home. Large numbers of women from poorer homes turned up both riddled with lice, and quite inadequately supplied with warm underclothing. Thus the Chief Controller issued a list of necessary articles strongly recommended as being essential for each member of the WAAC to possess before being drafted to a Unit. It read as follows:

1 pair strong shoes or boots (this of course being in addition to the free issue)
1 pr low-heeled shoes for housewear
2 prs khaki stockings (this of course being in addition to the free issue)
2 prs at least warm Combinations
2 prs dark coloured Knickers with washable linings
2 warm Vests of loosely woven Shetland wool
1 doz khaki Handkerchiefs
2 prs Pyjamas or 2 Strong Nightdresses
Burning Sanitary Towels
It is advisable if possible to bring as well, a Jersey or Golf Jacket which should be worn under the frock coat in cold weather.[42]

The WAAC was organized in four sections: Cookery, Mechanical, Clerical and Miscellaneous. It was repeated over and over again that no woman could be enrolled in the WAAC unless a soldier was thereby directly released for other purposes – though how this could be definitely established was another question. Four women clerks were to be considered as equivalent to three soldier clerks; and four technical women of the Royal Flying Corps and the Auxiliary Service Corps Motor Transport were to be considered as equivalent to three technical soldiers. In its publicity material the WAAC declared that 'In the WAAC women do all kinds of work which a woman can do as well as a man, and some which she can do better.' It continued: 'For instance most women can cook and do domestic work better than a man and every woman wants the armies to be well fed.' As the visual evidence brings out, women in uniform were often still performing the traditional feminine chores.

Embattled Ladies

The establishment of the WAAC intensified the problems of Mrs Furse and the Women's VAD organization. Mrs Furse was all in favour of very close cooperation between the VADs and the WAAC though, undoubtedly, she would herself have preferred to have been at the head of the combined operation. Actually it became clear that Mrs Furse and her organization

Women's Army Auxiliary Corps clerks in the central registry, Roux, 24 July 1917

were more and more being squeezed between Sir Arthur Stanley of the Red Cross on one side, and War Office on the other. The War Office insisted on taking responsibility for the welfare of VADs in military hospitals which meant, Mrs Furse rightly felt, that the justifiable grievances of many VADs serving in France were simply not being considered. Many influential members of the Government would have liked to have overruled Sir Arthur Stanley and see the VADs absorbed in the WAAC: but such absorption Mrs Furse herself was not prepared to tolerate. She actually threatened to withdraw her cooperation in the VAD general service scheme. She tried to maintain the separate appeal of the VADs in competition with that of the WAAC, revealingly making the point that 'VAD work is entirely for the sick and wounded. All such work is eminently the work of women.'

Her difficulties, especially with the Central Joint VAD Committee, intensified after June 1917. On 1 November 1917 Sir Arthur Stanley hastily called a special meeting of the Central Joint Committee whose purpose, quite simply, was to push Mrs Furse out, on the grounds that she had followed a policy of cooperation with the WAAC contrary to that of the Committee. Mrs Furse was indeed arguing for a 'big women's organization' to be under the nominal headship of Queen Mary: but although the Minutes of the meeting recorded the acceptance of Katherine Furse's resignation, Mrs Furse in fact refused to go.[43] Eventually she did go, but not before creating a considerable public furore which created a definite impression of bigoted and fuddy duddy men hindering an active and dedicated woman. In private Mrs Furse wrote to the leading feminist, Maud E. Royden.

... I think the only way in which you could help would be by telling women who are interested in women that in spite of an almost ceaseless struggle we have not succeeded in convincing the Red Cross and Order of St John that it is advisable that the Welfare and Control of women VAD members should be vested in women VAD officers, and not in men throughout the country.

They are old-fashioned enough to think that the masculine is more worthy than the feminine, and perhaps the fact that the charity element must necessarily exist in the Red Cross Society, and that, therefore, women's sphere is practically limited to that of 'ladies bountiful' is at the root of what I believe will soon cause the ruin of our Organization.[44]

There was sympathy and support for Mrs Furse, and also, of course, a good deal of rivalry between politicians and among different Service personnel. It was decided to set up a separate Royal Air Force, and also, first of all, to set up a Naval analogue of the WAAC, the WRNS, and then subsequently a Women's Royal Auxiliary Airforce. With little fuss, Mrs Furse was conciliated by being made Commandant-in-Chief of the new WRNS. Ironically, shortly afterwards, in April 1918, the WAAC formally became Queen Mary's Army Auxiliary Corps. The main effect was to run up a large stationery bill, since all the old headed notepaper had to be abandoned and new paper with the new title substituted.

Meantime, both Lady Londonderry, founder of the Women's Legion, and Mrs Chalmers Watson, first Chief Controller of the WAAC were also in the wars. Lady Londonderry was no longer immune to Government pressure to merge the Women's Legion with the WAAC, and Mrs Watson, as a medical woman, was naturally particularly interested in the formation of the Auxiliary Corps of the RAMC to be instituted as the Medical Services of the WAAC. It was agreed with the War Office that there should be two woman appointees, a President of the Medical Boards in England, and a Medical Controller in France. It was further agreed that both should have rank equivalent to Lieutenant-Colonel in the RAMC. A Lieutenant-Colonel in the RAMC had £700 per annum plus considerable allowances, including an allowance for his horse; yet when Dr Laura Sandeman was appointed Medical Controller in France, and Dr Isabel Cameron was seconded for three months from the local Government Board to be President of the Medical Boards in England, the Finance Department of the War Office refused to pay either of them more than £420, although both women were already earning more than £700 each. Dr Laura Sandeman simply refused to take up the appointment, while Dr Cameron did carry on, though hundreds of pounds out of pocket. When Mrs Chalmers Watson went to see the Permanent Financial Secretary of the War Office, Sir Charles Harris, about the salaries, his response was that patriotic ladies could always be found to do the work for less than men. Mrs Chalmers Watson replied that women with technical and professional qualifications were simply unable to make this sacrifice, and then went to see Sir Henry Foster at the Treasury who shared her views.

A conference then took place between Lord Derby, Sir Auckland Geddes, General Childs (Director of Personnel Services) and Mrs Chalmers Watson, and it was laid down that 'technical' women should be paid at the rate of the men they replaced. Mrs Chalmers Watson considered the question now settled, but the Finance Department of the War Office again intervened saying that Lord Derby had no right to interfere and refused to sanction the salaries.

Women air mechanics of the Women's Royal Air Force working on the fuselage of an Avro biplane

Accordingly, Dr Sandeman maintained her refusal to go to France, so that Lord Derby's hand was forced. His petulant reaction was that: 'I am between the devil and the deep blue sea. On the one hand, I consider it outrageous that no medical woman will accept an appointment under £700 a year. On the other hand I cannot obtain a Medical Service for the WAAC in France and I am therefore obliged to agree to this salary, but I strongly recommend that neither of the two ladies in question should be given the appointment.'

An Army Council instruction then appeared founding an Auxiliary Corps of the RAMC. This laid down that the head officers should be paid £700 a year, with a uniform allowance and that all subordinate medical officers should get 24/6 a day, a civilian doctor's rate. Women were still at a slight disadvantage compared with male officers in the RAMC in that their pensions were not of equivalent value and they still paid Income Tax on a civilian basis. Travel concessions, a long standing grievance within the WAAC, were poor. However, said Mrs Watson, 'on the whole the struggle ended in a victory for the women.'[45] It was agreed that the Controller of Medical Services in France should wear a rose and fleurs de lys corresponding to the star and crown of the Lieutenant-Colonel, and that all the badges of the service were graded upwards and downwards to correspond with the Army grading. In the end, the status of the women in the RAMC Auxiliary Corps was considerably superior to the status of

women doctors in the military hospitals in France, who continued to have lower rates and no uniform. But the struggle was an exhausting one for Mrs Watson, and in February 1918 she resigned as Chief Controller, being succeeded by Mrs Burleigh Leach.

There was one other *cause célèbre*. The Hon. Violet Douglas-Pennant had been appointed First Commandant of the Women's Royal Air Force. Almost from the beginning she complained of obstruction by male officers; and she also fell foul of her assistant Commandant, Katherine Andrew. She did not even resign, but had her appointment terminated. The entire correspondence surrounding this event was considered so important that it was published as a parliamentary blue book.

What Was It Like?

There was, as the language of the day had it, to be no 'social intercourse' between Administrators and rank and file in the WAAC, nor, more critically, between officers in the army, and rank and file members of the WAAC or VAD. No doubt the latter regulation was as much honoured in the breach as in the observance, but, as we shall see, there were all sorts of curtailments on the freedom of all members of the various uniformed women's organizations.

At the end of 1975, a former member compiled these 'Memoirs of a WAAC'.

> In the Spring of 1917 an announcement appeared in the National newspapers to the effect that a Women's Army Auxiliary Corps was to be formed, and soliciting applications for recruits of 21 years of age and over for service at home and abroad. The categories were Shorthand typists, Clerks, Telephonists and Household. The pay was to be 37/6d per week for Shorthand Typists, 27/6d per week for Clerks, all less 14/- per week for board and laundry etc. As these were the categories which interested me I naturally applied for the former.
> Recruiting Headquarters for my district was Birmingham. I made my application on the first day the advertisement appeared, but received

a reply that the quota for Shorthand Typists had already been filled locally. As my home was some 16 miles from Headquarters I wrote again and offered my services in the Clerical Section. It was some time before I received a reply, and on 10 May I was asked to appear before a Selection and Medical Board in Birmingham. I was passed fit, and on the 14 July I received a letter indicating that I had been accepted as a Shorthand Typist for service abroad, and giving instructions to join a certain train and proceed to Aldershot for training. When I entered the reserved carriage on the train I found all the girls had similar passes and were bound for the same destination.

We were asked to bring an overcoat or raincoat as none were available at the time. We were met in London and escorted to the train for Aldershot. Our training Headquarters was a large country house in Farnborough, very near to a R. Flying Corps Camp. There were around 200 girls in training at the time. This included the routine we would be expected to follow, i.e. drill, lectures, etc. On one or two occasions we were invited to a concert in the RFC Camp, which made a nice change and which we enjoyed very much. Whilst in Farnborough we were vaccinated and inoculated twice, and were issued with a one-piece dress, a pair of stiff army shoes, and two pairs of thick khaki stockings. We had to supply our own underwear as there was never any issued.

We were split up in groups and in less than a month we were trained for our respective bases in France. We must have looked a queer cargo, all shapes and sizes, as we were obliged to wear lifebelts for the crossing as the Channel was mined. We spent the night in a large hut on the banks of the river in Boulogne. The following day I was amongst a group put on the train for Etaples, which at that time was a large Reinforcement Base. After a very slow journey and a great many enquiries at each stop we eventually arrived at Etaples and were met by a WAAC Officer. We were marched to the Camp which was situated on a hill a short distance from the Station, and was the dividing line between the Village and the Reinforcement Camp. Our camp was composed of Nissen and long wooden huts. I was allocated a bed along with about 19 other girls and one NCO who had a small compartment of her own, in one of the wooden huts which were reserved for the Shorthand Typists and Clerks. The telephonists were housed in the smaller Nissen huts, which were more convenient for split duties. The beds were composed of hard mattresses and a pillow and two rough dark blankets. Each morning before going to work we had to fold the blankets and place them with the pillow at the bottom of the bed. It wasn't very comfortable sleeping without sheets, but I eventually wangled a nice white blanket to the envy of many of the other girls.

On arrival at the Camp we were assembled in the drill hall and given the 'gen' on Camp life. Much to my surprise we were informed that we could make friends with the troops, but were advised to choose carefully. I had not anticipated that this would be allowed, but like many other girls it was here that I was to meet my future husband. We were split up into little groups and sent to different Regimental Base Depots to work with the existing staff. Two other girls and myself were sent to one Depot in charge of a dear old Colonel – one of the real old Brigade who didn't believe in making the girls work. However, eventually we took over, thereby releasing the troops for other duties.

On our first Sunday in Etaples, the Sergeant Major, who was old enough to be our Father, volunteered to escort the three of us to Paris-Plage, now the popular seaside resort of Le Touquet. A small train with open trailers ran to Paris-Plage, but the Sergeant Major decided to walk through the woods, which were delightful, and a very proud man indeed he was to be escorting three young ladies. Needless to say this was his only opportunity as we very soon found friends of our own age. We usually spent our free time in Paris-Plage, generally for the purpose of having a feast of egg and chips and luscious French pastries which could always be bought when funds allowed. We were given a small hut attached to the office for our personal use.

Whilst serving in that Infantry Base Depot I celebrated my 21st Birthday. I am afraid I told a little white lie to enable me to enlist, as at that time I was under the required age. We decided to have a little tea-party and invite the office staff. I had expected a parcel of 'eats' from home, but up to mid-day on my birthday it had not arrived. Consequently a hurried trip to Paris-Plage was indicated to buy cakes etc. When we returned to Camp the parcel had arrived, so we were able to have quite a 'tuck-in'.

We were encouraged to contribute towards the building of a YWCA hut in our own Camp where we could invite and entertain our friends of both sexes. This proved highly successful, and was the nearest thing to home. We even had cups and saucers, not exactly china, but very superior to our usual tin mugs. It was run by Members of the YWCA and was luxury indeed to our Camp life. Roll Call was at 9.00 p.m. each night, but if we were working late we had to produce a pass from the office, I hardly need mention this was inclined to be mis-used, as it was not always strictly work. One night I missed the last tram from Paris-Plage and consequently could not be in Camp for Roll Call. To my horror an electric light had been installed in the entrance outside the Orderly Room and it was impossible to avoid being seen. Naturally I was caught and told to report to the officer in charge of the Clerical Section the next morning. This I duly did and explained my reason for being late. Our Officer was a motherly type and just said 'run away child and don't do it again'. I had expected as a punishment to be 'confined to Camp' for a few days.

After some months the Infantry Base Depots were reorganized and I was transferred to another office. This was not a very happy change. Although the Colonel was a very nice man one or two junior officers appeared to resent our presence. During the great retreat we were obliged to work very long hours and it was often around midnight when we returned to Camp. The troops were flowing back from the Front in great numbers to the Base Depot to be re-equipped, given new regimental numbers and transferred to new units to form complete regiments, and then returned to the Front Line.

The German Air Force had commenced attacking the Base and a working party were detailed to make a trench outside each hut in our Camp, of which we were all to occupy as soon as the alarm sounded, taking a blanket with us and remain there until the 'all clear'. The trenches were without any cover and were totally inadequate to accommodate all the girls. Girls who were not nervous would remain in bed, occasionally to be unceremoniously chased out if the huts were inspected by the officers. Later, as the bombing increased it became evident that other shelter was necessary, and a trench was made at the bottom of the Camp through a field and led into chalk caves. The trench was covered at intervals by sheets of corrugated iron, and we ran from one to the other dodging the shrapnel which clattered on the corrugated iron until we reached the entrance to the caves. We were allocated one part and the French villagers had access to another part. The caves were situated on the banks of the River Canche and were alleged to be where Napoleon sheltered his troops. The white chalk of the caves, lit here and there by a solitary candle presented a weird appearance. As the bombing grew worse it was decided that one third of the camp should sleep there each night, taking it in turns in order to avoid confusion on the alarm being given. Each girl was advised to take a blanket and settle down for the night. The firing of a gun nearby sounded the alarm, and it was a work of art for the other two thirds of the girls to pick their way through the sleepers and find a suitable spot. Needless to say the chalk floor was no substitute for even the army beds, but as we were young we were able to cope. The raids took place mostly at night, the approach in the daytime being too risky. Occasionally there would be fights between planes within a short distance of the camp. The girls did not appreciate the danger and invariably went outside to watch much to the consternation of the officers who insisted on our taking cover.

One dawn, after a very bad night we were assembled in the field outside the caves and informed that the Camp had received direct hits and some of the huts had been demolished. We were instructed to gather what possessions we could find and join another hut until further arrangements could be made. Our YWCA hut had entirely disappeared, which grieved us very much. Scraps of the furniture etc. including our much prized piano were scattered over the Parade ground. The dining room was a little more fortunate, being left standing with an odd wall or two but no roof. Our hut was more or less habitable. In each hut there was a little shelf where the roof overlapped the sides and we used to hide such things as tea, sugar, milk, etc. plus a small primus stove used for our small culinary efforts. Everything had been shaken off the shelf and the Camp cat was blissfully having a feast of tinned milk. During these raids the hospitals were badly bombed resulting in many casualties. A yacht was moored at the mouth of the River Canche, for the purpose, we understood of taking on the VIPs in the event of evacuation of Northern France by the Allies.

An unfortunate incident happened towards the end of the summer of 1917. Military Police were stationed at the entrance to the Camps. One Sunday evening a New Zealand soldier was standing talking to one of the girls and apparently was slightly over the Camp Boundary line. He was ordered back by a Military Policeman but appeared to resent the order. An argument followed and the Policeman drew his revolver and fired. Unfortunately the bullet hit and killed a Highland Light Infantry soldier leaving the Camp Cinema. This caused a riot with the result that the Policeman was beaten up and dropped from the Railway Bridge into a wagon of a passing train bound for Boulogne. After this event an order was issued that all girls on late duty were to be escorted back to Camp until all the trouble had subsided.

During my stay in Etaples I met quite a number of boys from my home town, including, in the first week, my next door neighbour. He was in Etaples for one night on the way to the front line.

During the severe spell in the winter of 1917 the water pipes were all frozen. We used to collect a mug full of snow and place it on the stove in the dining room whilst we had breakfast, then pass it round for whatever kind of wash we could manage.

There was quite a bit of talent in Camp and the girls formed a Concert Party. I was persuaded to join a friend in a little dance for two. I had no knowledge of stage dancing but soon fell into the routine, and we perfected the act in time for the Concert. Alas on the day it was to be held my partner fell ill, and in order not to let the programme down I was faced with a solo act. I hate to think what it was like, but the troops appeared to approve. I must admit that it was my one and only solo appearance. We had a very good soprano in the party and one of her numbers was 'The Pipes of Pan'. As she was in the middle of the trills a gruff voice from the back of the hall shouted 'Get it off your chest, Miss', much to the amusement of the audience and the embarassment of the singer.[46]

We also have this reminiscence of life with the VADs in France:

In 1917 at the age of 19, I joined the VAD and without any experience of nursing was sent to France.

My first post was at the Hotel Bristol in Boulogne where I was put to work in a vast underground scullery, where we stood on duck-boards because there was so much water on the floor, to say nothing of the rats.

4 of us were set to work on the revolting job of cutting off the green fat from the carcasses (beef and mutton) which by the time they arrived at the Hotel, which was the HQ of the VAD were more than ready for the oven! This fat was used in the manufacture of muni-tions we were given to understand. At times there would be a shout of 'Le Fleming, someone to see you' and without a chance to wash off the soot and grease one would climb the stone steps to be greeted by some friend who one had last seen in more glamorous circumstances and, alas! whom one would probably never see again; sometimes it would be less than a week when we would get the news of 'death in action' or 'missing, believed killed'.

After 2 months in Boulogne I was drafted to Le Treport in Normandy; there were 5 hospitals here on the cliff overlooking the sea.

I was, with 2 other girls, sent to work in the kitchens of a hostel where 40 women ambulance drivers lived. None of the 3 of us knew much about cooking, indeed one girl had never even boiled an egg! However we muddled through and there were good little restaurants open in the bay so the drivers occasionally went out to avoid starvation.

Apart from the kitchen work, we had to go at night with the drivers to meet the trains bringing the wounded and the next morning at 11.00 a.m. 2 of us would attend the burials – I can never forget those lines of coffins covered with the Union Jack.

There were bright moments when friends got down from the line for a 48 hour leave and with another girl as chaperone as we were never allowed out by ourselves, we would bathe – it was the summer of 1917 – and lunch, with someone near the door to see that the

Queen Mary's Army Auxiliary Corps Camp in the Forest of Crécy, 7 June 1918

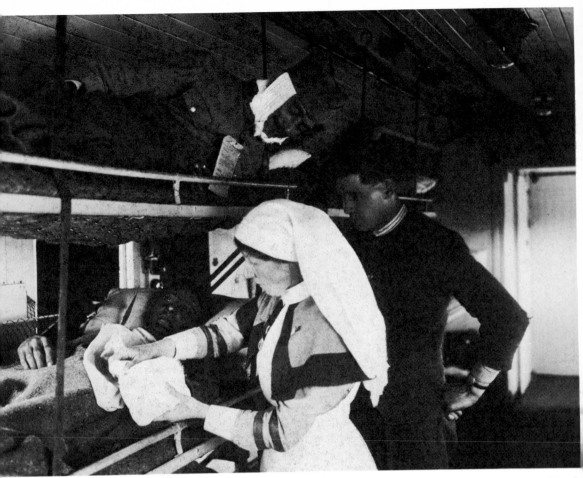

British ambulance train near Doullens, 27 April 1918. French and British casualties from the German offensive in Flanders having their wounds dressed

Commandant was not about! Dame Crowdy, we were terrified of her! One day I was taken in an ambulance to Etaples, but before we got there the air-raid began which caused so many casualties in the many hospitals. I well remember lying in a ditch, watching the planes as the bombs fell.[47]

What this, like so many other accounts glosses over, was the trauma of trying to minister to men who were not just dead and dying, but frequently suffering from the most horrifying mutilations, the product of a war in which too often mere flesh and blood was pitted against all the fiendish machinery of modern military technology.

A different touch is added by this complaint from the father of a VAD who had been invalided home after two years' service in military hospitals in France. At the time of his letter, 15 June 1917, she was working in Queen Mary's Military Hospital, Whalley, Lancashire, and being treated as a mere probationer: 'She complains that the men are very free-making, and she is constantly subjected to unwelcome attentions from the wounded soldiers. In other respects also the conditions are not congenial, as she finds herself out of sympathy with the points of view of most of the other Nursing Sisters, who do not appear to make allowances for those whose natural inclinations and upbringing compel them to resent incidents which the majority appear to accept as usual.'[48] But perhaps it is necessary to add that father and daughter hailed from Dublin.

Finally, an illuminating but perhaps rather sad, insight into the motives which led some girls to enlist in the WAAC is contained in this circular from the WAAC Headquarters on the subject of discharges on compassionate grounds. Dated 22 January 1918, it says that no discharges on compassionate grounds can be given for: enrolling in a fit of temper; enrolling without taking into due consideration the fact that the member has enrolled for the duration of the war; enrolling without parents' knowledge.[49]

Questions of Discipline

The Women's Land Army, for agricultural work at home, came into formal existence at the same time as the WAAC. It succeeded in boosting the total number of women working on the land to 113,000 in July 1918, compared with 80,000 in July 1914. The Land Army was divided into three sections; agricultural; timber cutting; and forage. For the first two sections, a woman could enrol for a minimum of either six or twelve months; for the forage section, which was more closely associated with home army camps, since it provided forage for army horses, minimum terms were one year, and the contract of employment was much more strict. Other organizations providing similar services continued to exist, for example the Women's Forestry Corps, which was directly under the Board of Trade, and the Forage Corps. In the Land Army, women were given a minimum wage, with additional payments depending on the number of days actually worked.

The Women's Land Army Handbook, issued to all members, laid down the basic principle in regard to appearance and deportment: 'You are doing a man's work and so you're dressed rather like a man, but remember just because you wear a smock and breeches you should take care to behave like a British girl who expects chivalry and respect from everyone she meets.'

However much some women may have regretted enlisting for overseas service, at least they did have the excitement of a completely new environment and of a sense of direct participation in the military effort. By 1918 war weariness was quite widespread on the Home Front, and in such domestic uniformed organizations as the Women's Land Army much of the initial sense of purpose, inevitably, had evaporated. In the Departmental Records there is a whole file on 'Women's Land Army: Need for more effective control'.[50] Partly this was again a matter of class: upper-class people resenting the behaviour of the working-class girls who were increasingly being recuited into the Land Army. There are many letters asking for discipline, and a tighter code of conduct, particularly with reference to girls going into public houses, being out of their billets after 9.30 p.m., failing to wear their overalls at all times, and fraternizing with German prisoners of war. The Women's Branch of the Board of Agriculture Food Production Department had to point out that the Land Army was not really an army: there could be no question of Draconian discipline.

In June 1918 an internal Food Production Department Minute noted that 'The supply of girls of sufficiently high character to make it safe to send them out to live alone on the farms or in cottages is running short'. Thus it was decided to appoint a special team of welfare officers. Many regarded this as a soft response. The nature of the controversy is best expressed in the language of the time, and can be seen clearly in this letter of 4 July 1918 from Lady Mather Jackson, Chairman of the Ladies' Committee of Monmouthshire War Agricultural Committee, to Miss Talbot of the Food Production Department of the Board of Agriculture.

LEFT Member of the Women's
Land Army working with
dairy cattle
BELOW Member of the
Women's Land Army
ploughing. The horses look as
though they are already
feeling the food shortages

Members of the Women's
Forage Department of the
Land Army feeding a
hay baler

ear Miss Talbot,

am venturing to write to you on the question of Control and
iscipline of the Land Army Girls, as we feel here that it is a very
nportant and serious question, and that we as an Army are so very
r behind both the WAAC and the WRENS [sic]. In respect of this. I
m hoping that you will be able to help us in this matter.

When Girls join up they have the Rules read to them and are
arned as to their responsibilities and duties both at the Training
entre and also to their Employers after training. The great diffi-
lty that we have is, that the Girls are constantly asking for week-
nds off, and their opposition to the order with regard to their time
f coming in at night, also their general behaviour when off duty.
hey stay out late and often do not return to their Farms until 12
nd one in the morning. This is of constant occurrence if they are
ithin distance of a Town, and naturally they are very much talked
bout. The Girls, themselves, with few exceptions, do the least
ossible work they can, and knowing that their hours are fixed, they
ever if they can help it oblige by working late, although it is clearly

understood that overtime is paid for according to the custom of the District. We have had cases lately of the Girls running away from the Training Centres after working two or three days, also of Girls leaving the Farm, which in every way are very satisfactory, except that they are in the Country and 'far from the madding Crowd'.

Now that we have Gang Hostels, I suggested at a Meeting of our Committee a fortnight ago that Girls behaving in this way, should be sent to these Hostels for a fortnight, doing work from there, and not being allowed to go out after working hours in that time, in short 'being confined to Barracks' for so many days according to their misbehaviour. I am however told that this would not be approved of by the Board, but I do feel that we ought to be able to have a stronger hold on the Girls than we have at the present time. No doubt we have here an absolutely different Class of Girls to deal with than in most Country Districts as they are drawn from Industrial-Centres and from Colliery Districts, where they have been under no control or discipline whatever, and have been brought up to do practically nothing, their Fathers earning big Wages as Colliers.

It is very disheartening to all of us to find that after two years the Farmers are still very loathe to employ the Girls which I feel sure is due to their lack of discipline.

I am venturing to forward you herewith a Card of Rules which we have drawn up for our Training Centres and Hostels in the hope of installing [sic] in the minds of the Girls during their training method and orderliness in their work and conduct.

I do not know whether you have seen the enclosed, which appears to be somewhat stiff judgement, but on the other hand, I think that a few Girls brought before the Magistrates for example, would perhaps make them realize better their responsibilities.

The enclosure was this quite scarifying newspaper cutting:

GAOL FOR LAND ARMY WOMAN

Grace Smith, a native of Bristol, and belonging to the Women's Army Forage Department, was at Gloucester on Friday sent to prison for fourteen days' hard labour for being absent from work without leave.

Lady Mather-Jackson also enclosed her 'Rules for Training Centre' These ran to fourteen in all, and included the following:

The Pupils must immediately on arrival report themselves to the Principal;

The use of improper language, rowdy behaviour, or inattention to Rules, will be considered sufficient reason for expulsion;

All Pupils must attend some place of Worship on Sunday mornings unless prevented by their Farm Duties;

Pupils must carry out any form of practical or manual work that may be demanded at such time and places as may be required; and:

Pupils must take Notes at Lectures and keep a record of the work done. These Notes must be in legible form and properly arranged and must be handed in for inspection when required.

The timetable to which Pupils had to adhere strictly, was:

Rise 6.00 a.m. Breakfast, 6.45 a.m., Dinner, 12.15 p.m. Tea, 6.00 p.m. Bedtime-Summer, 9.30 p.m. Bedtime-Winter 9.00 p.m.

After these horrors, the reply from Miss Talbot of the Food Production Department, shows a woman Civil Servant of the period at her most sensitive and caring. Once again, Miss Talbot had to point out that the Land Army was not really an army, and that the girls were working for private employers. She continued:

> It is, as I have no doubt you will realize, the experience of those most competent to judge that with all young people the best results are achieved when the fewest rules are in force. I am inclined to think that the rules for the Training Centre which you sent me are somewhat over-elaborate, but no doubt you have special difficulties . . .
>
> The kind of extreme discipline and penalty evidenced by that case at Gloucester in accordance with the Forage Section Regulations does not, in my opinion, lead to desirable results, indeed such severe punishment besides bringing great discredit upon the young woman perhaps for life, is also likely to do much serious harm, and is to be deprecated.

Heroines of War

The significant part played by Scots, men as well as women, in the struggle for women's rights deserves some attention. Certainly Scotland offered greater educational opportunities to women and in Scotland the drive to egalitarianism and democracy was rather stronger than in England, with its upper-class ladies and voluntary organizations. In August 1914, Dr Hector Munro, a Scotsman, raised a flying ambulance corps to go to the assistance of the hard-pressed Belgian Army. Since he was a leading feminist, he decided to include four women in his team, in order that they might prove their worth by going on to the battlefields under fire. The team consisted of two English women, Lady Dorothy Fielding and Mrs Knocker, one American, Mrs Helen Gleason, who were all in their twenties, and one eighteen-year-old Scots girl, Mairi Chisholm.

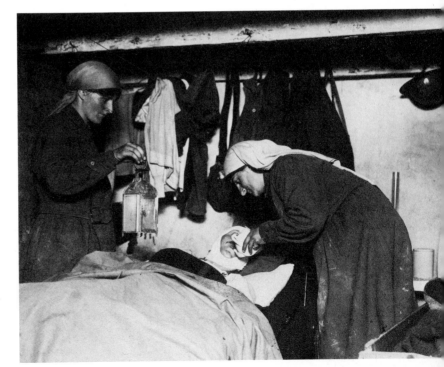

The two women of Pervyse: Baroness de T'Serclaes and Miss Mairi Chisholm attending to a wounded Belgian soldier in one of their advanced dressing posts, 6 August 1917

ABOVE Scottish Women's Hospitals on the Balkan front. Driver fixing a wheel to her motor ambulance
OPPOSITE Elsie Maud Inglis

honour of Nurse Edith Cavell. Working with the Red Cross in German-occupied Belgium, Edith Cavell, had nursed British, Belgian and German soldiers, but because she had helped allied soldiers to escape, she was court-martialled by the Germans, and, despite the energetic efforts of the American Embassy, hastily shot. Technically, the Germans did have something of a case, but it was a case which completely failed to commend itself to world opinion. Naturally, British propaganda abroad and at home (including film propaganda) made the most of the incident. More important from the point of view of the question of women's rights, was Asquith's declaration:

> She has taught the bravest man amongst us a supreme lesson of courage; and in this United Kingdom and through the Dominions of the Crown there are thousands of such women, but a year ago we did not know it.

Heroines were to be found nearer home. Explosions at munitions factories killed a total of 71 women munition workers. Sixty-one women died of poisoning and other fatal accidents killed eighty-one women. Inevitably, and perhaps quite properly, the dangers run by women munition workers received less prominence than the individualistic exploits of women under fire. The Government, in any case, suppressed all information on the exact location of munitions factories.

The vicious terms of combat on the Western Front, of course, called forth from men incredible acts of bravery. Thus in March 1916, a new decoration, the Military Medal was created. This was thrown open to women in

June 1916, the first award in July 1916, being made to a French Nurse, Mlle E. Moreau 'for gallantry'. The first English woman to win the Military Medal was the same Lady Dorothy Fielding who had gone out with the women of Pervyse 'for bravery as an ambulance driver'. Thereafter, a number of nurses won the medal, and it is interesting to note that two awards were made for bravery under fire during the Irish rebellion of Easter 1916. Perhaps because they had already received their important Belgian honours, the women of Pervyse did not get the Military Medal until 1917. The first woman to be mentioned in despatches was Miss D. Eden for bravery while nursing in January 1917, followed by a further six nurses in February 1917. In June 1917, King George, wishing to recognize other sorts of distinguished service, created two new orders: the Order of the British Empire, and the Order of the Companions of Honour. From the start these were open to men and women alike.

The Medal of the Order of the British Empire was handed out fairly lavishly to women factory workers. The ceremonies were always worth a column or two in the local press:

> Of those thus honoured the little girl in a white dress and with a pink bow-tie in her hair (Miss Dolly Gladys Vickers of 3, Carleton Place, Aberdeen Street, Birmingham), was naturally the most arresting figure. She looked younger than her sixteen years, and when Mr E. Field (Clerk to the Lieutenancy), who was attired in wig and gown, recited the . . . particulars of her brave act, she blushed at finding herself rendered famous . . .

The Liberal MP Thomas Kellaway spoke in Parliament of the bravery of six girl transport workers who helped to extinguish a fire in a London munitions factory. All the girls had previously been parlour-maids or housemaids. Miss Kate Shepherd, formerly in service at a hotel in Tunbridge Wells, gave this account:

> I was doing some crochet work in my tea time when I heard the alarm. In my hurry to get to the fire I ran over an allotment and fell into a ditch. We had to push through a crowd of men who shouted to us not to go near. The exploding cartridges were making a fearful noise. Most of us were struck by bullets but only bruised; there was not much power in the hits. We still kept our hoses in action after the firemen arrived, working at one end of the shed while the firemen were at the other.[52]

After a big factory explosion in the North of England women employees behaved with such coolness that it was announced that Sir Douglas Haig was to be asked to let the men at the Front know of the courage and discipline of their women folk.

From the beginning the Great War was a war of the whole British Empire against Germany; from May 1917, it was a war involving the United States of America. Acts of bravery by nurses from the White Dominions and from America were frequently noted. Let this privately printed account of the sinking of His Majesty's hospital ship *Llandovery Castle*, destroyed at sea by enemy action on 27 June 1918, speak for many. Only six of the total hospital personnel of ninety-seven survived.

> Through it all nothing stands out more brilliantly than the coolness and courage of the fourteen Canadian nursing sisters, every one of whom was lost, and whose sacrifice under the conditions about to

be described will serve to inspire throughout the whole Empire a yet fuller sense of appreciation of the deep debt of gratitude this nation owes to the nursing service.

At the outset it is well to consider the circumstances unwhich which these fourteen nurses were engaged on hospital ship duty.

Five of them volunteered for service at the very outbreak of hostilities in 1914, and came to England and France with the first Canadian division, six had seen active service in casualty clearing stations in France throughout the intervening period, four had been with the Canadian hospitals at Salonica, three had been mentioned in despatches, and most of them had been recently transferred to transport duty by way of change, and what would, under ordinary conditions prove a rest.

For many months, and, in some cases, two years, these sisters had endured the hazards of the shelled areas in France, splendidly contributing to the efficiency of the Medical Service. (No less, it may be added, than six out of the fourteen had been at casualty clearing stations within the 'shell zone' immediately behind the Front.) How magnificently they faced the final ordeal on that awful evening of 27 June is simply, yet graphically related in the Story of Sergeant A. Knight, the non-commissioned officer of the CAMC, who took charge of lifeboat No. 5, into which the fourteen nurses were placed.

'Our boat,' said Sergeant Knight, 'was quickly loaded and lowered to the surface of the water. Then the crew of eight men and myself faced the difficulty of getting free from the ropes holding us to the ship's side. I broke two axes trying to cut ourselves away, but was unsuccessful.'

With the forward motion and choppy sea the boat all the time was pounding against the ship's side. To save the boat we tried to keep ourselves away by using the oars, and soon all of them were broken. Finally the ropes became loose at the top and we commenced to drift away. We were carried towards the stern of the ship, when suddenly the poop-deck seemed to break away and sink. The suction drew us quickly into the vacuum, the boat tipped over sideways, and every occupant went under.

I estimate we were together in the boat about eight minutes. In that whole time I did not hear a complaint or a murmur from one of the sisters. They were supremely calm and collected. Everyone was perfectly conscious. There was not a cry for help or any untoward evidence of fear. In the entire time I overhead only one remark, when the matron, Nursing Sister M. M. Frazer, turned to me as we drifted helplessly towards the stern of the ship and asked: 'Sergeant, do you think there is any hope for us?'

I replied, 'No,' seeing myself our helplessness with oars and the sinking condition of the stern of the ship.

A few seconds later we were drawn into the whirl-pool of the submerged after-deck, and the last I saw of the nursing sisters was they were thrown over the side of the boat. All were wearing life-belts, and of the fourteen two were in their night dress, the others in uniform.

'It was,' concluded Sergeant Knight, 'doubtful if any of them came to the surface again, although I myself sank and came up three times, finally clinging to a piece of wreckage, and being eventually picked up by the Captain's boat.'

Damage done during air raids on hospital area, Etaples. Photograph taken on 2 June 1918 showing site of No. 9 Canadian Stationary Hospital, bombed on night of 31 May 1918

To hundreds of officers and men of the Canadian overseas forces the name of Nursing Sister Miss Margaret Margerie ('Pearl') Frazer will recall a record of unselfish effort, a fitting tribute to the Nation's womanhood.

Volunteering for active service in the CAMC, on 29 September 1914, Miss Frazer went to France with the First Canadian division, and for almost three years had been on duty in casualty clearing stations.

In that time not a few of her patients had been German wounded. Many times had she been the first to give a drink of water to these parched enemy casualties. Many a time had she written down the dying statements of enemy officers and men, transmitting them to their relatives through the Red Cross organization.

Her faithfulness was only typical, however, of that service for humanity exhibited by everyone of these precious fourteen lives sacrificed in this latest act of Hunnish barbarity.[53]

Inevitably the propaganda message was drawn; but there was that other message as well. When the hospital ship *Anglia* was sunk in November 1916, the nurses insisted on giving up their life-belts to the wounded soldiers being ferried home: *Votes for Women* produced a front page cartoon calling for '*Votes for Heroines as well as Heroes*' (See page 152).

Women civilians were at risk from enemy air raids. Altogether between January 1915, and April 1918, there were 51 Zeppeling raids, causing 1,913 casualties: and between December 1914 and June 1918, there were 57 aeroplane raids, causing 2,907 casualties. Total civilian fatalities were 1,570, though the exact proportion of women is not known.

Nurses and WAACs in France quite far behind the lines, ran the risk of attack by long distance shells, as well as bombing from the air. At Abbeville on 29 and 30 May 1918, nine WAAC workers were killed by bombs, and next day several nurses were killed at Etaples.

General Plumer decorating
women ambulance drivers for
bravery during air raids,
Blendecques, 3 July 1918

CHAPTER FIVE

MANNERS, MORALS AND MENUS

1914–1918

War Babies

Feminists very properly object to the way in which sexual morality is often treated as pertaining to women alone. The changes in sexual attitudes, and the less manifest changes in sexual behaviour of the war period, naturally affected men as well as women. However, in the context of an age in which the Edwardian double-standard still persisted and when constraints on women were more severe than those on men, questions of sexual morality undoubtedly did have a special relevance for women. This was indeed recognized at the time by activists in the women's movement whose conferences discussed questions of venereal diseases, prostitution, illegitimacy and sex education when such matters were largely ignored by male-dominated organizations.

The main factors affecting sexual behaviour in general, and that of women in particular, can be summarized as: religious and social restraints, threatening transgressors with punishments ranging from eternal damnation to social ostracism; fear of physical consequences, such as venereal disease and pregnancy – the latter, obviously affecting women more than men: opportunity – the war, obviously, took both men and women out of their sheltered family environments. For what it was worth, chaperons had disappeared too: they were, as one young lady explained, 'Hard at work canteening and so on, and people who gave parties did not want to feed and water them. And if they were elderly, they didn't feel like having to walk home after late nights.' Finally there is the very important question of modesty and innocence – whereas today many girls and boys discuss sexual matters quite openly with each other, at the time of the First World War very large numbers of girls, and quite a lot of boys as well, were (as it would seem to us today) remarkably innocent and hedged about by a deep sense of personal modesty.

Apart from inducing shifts in standards and behaviour, the upheavals of war also simply revealed, and perhaps even reinforced, existing prejudices and preconceptions. Among influential women as well as men, there was much concern over the danger to the moral welfare of women and girls brought about by the new conditions. Sometimes the assumption seems to have been that women were basically weak and gullible, sometimes that men were naturally predators simply looking for occasion and opportunity, sometimes a mixture of both. Hardened military men often took the cynical view that if you suddenly introduced women to areas where men had been isolated from their own womenfolk for considerable periods of time, you could expect only one consequence. To this must be added the apparently eternal predisposition of groups of men to fantasize, and indeed spread quite ill-founded rumours, about the moral behaviour of women. The roots of this – frustration, rejection, jealousy – need not detain us here, though some were, as we shall see, delicately explored by one Committee of Inquiry.

Whether the institution of the chaperon owed more to a genuine fear that if a girl were left alone with a man she would automatically succumb to his apparently irresistible charm, or simply to the convention that the remote possibility of this happening was enough to lose a girl her reputation, is a moot point. Certainly much of the first moral fuss after the war broke out was stirred up by some of the women's organizations, particularly the Women Patrols and the Women Police Service. Typically, as we have seen, the Women Patrols were concerned with such locations as 'a stretch of the sands and the foreshore which is badly spoken of, though not more so in these times than any other times', and with such individuals as 'bad women' who 'hang about the billets' under the pretext of doing the washing for the troops; and a characteristic activity for the Women's Police Service was reported by Woman Constable Morris on patrol in Greenwich Park: 'Noticed girl of 16 speak to four different soldiers, and go off with the last one. I then spoke to her, telling her she did not know the soldier; she let me see her to her bus for home quite willingly. I then went back and spoke to the soldier.'[54] One has an irresistible vision of the woman constable herself then going off with the soldier, but alas, I fear that would be hopelessly wishful thinking.

OPPOSITE ABOVE The grey uniformity of war time life. The specially built housing estate for munitions workers at Gretna
OPPOSITE BELOW Group of women munitions workers at Gretna
ABOVE Air raid damage, 63 Oval Road Croydon: airship raid of 13–14 October 1915

Girl guides taking wounded soldiers for a row

Next came the discovery in April 1915 of 'war babies'. In a letter to the *Morning Post*, which was extensively quoted and embellished in the rest of the press, a Conservative MP, Mr Ronald McNeill, announced that throughout the country, in districts where large numbers of troops had been quartered, 'a great number of girls' were about to become unmarried mothers. The stories were greatly exaggerated, for the year 1915 actually presented the highly moral combination of an exceptionally low illegitimate birth rate, and a phenomenally high marriage rate – though many of the marriages, no doubt, took place in some haste. In any case, the fantastic 1915 figure of 19.5 marriages per thousand inhabitants would, to the Edwardians, have suggested a lubricious disregard of the requirements of social security. Marriage in haste often meant divorce at leisure: there was nearly a three-fold increase in the number of divorces 'made absolute' between 1910 (596) and 1920 (1,629). Next year the illegitimacy rate did go up and by the end of the war, it was about 30 per cent up on pre-war figures.

Of course, illegitimacy statistics are no sure indicator of sexual activity. From a wealth of impressionistic evidence it does seem clear that there were changes in behaviour, related on the one hand to the new economic and social freedoms which women derived from their war work, and on the other, to the heightened emotional intensity generated by the war and the colossal slaughter of human life on the battlefields

118

especially since knowledge of mechanical methods of contraception was spreading, particularly when the troops were given a free issue as a prophylactic against venereal diseases.

In a report on conditions in Coventry towards the end of 1916, where there had been an influx of 9,000 women and 7,000 men, the eminently level-headed Misses Anderson and Markham concluded that they were 'unable to set aside the testimony' of immorality.[55] Young girls were often daily travelling long hours from home, or in many cases, had left home to live in hostels or lodgings of their own. Explaining the 1916 upsurge in the illegitimacy rate, the Registrar General referred to 'The exceptional circumstances of the year, including the freedom from home restraints of large numbers of young persons of both sexes.'

On the whole, there was a more sympathetic attitude towards the unmarried mother and her baby. 'The War Babies and Mothers' League' declared that 'The children of our soldiers and sailors *must* be cared for.' The Secretary of the League explained the moral situation as he saw it:

> In the majority of cases, it is simply a matter of a young girl and a young man losing their heads when the man is going off to the Front.[56]

A not dissimilar attitude is taken in the Pamphlet, *The Story of a Girl's Soul*, published in 1918, in support of the 'Mission of Hope' homes for unmarried mothers and their children:

> There came an hour when the youth pleaded and the girl yielded. She does not blame him. It is part of her honesty to tell you frankly that the fault was hers as much as his. She does not say 'he tempted me'. She says that for both of them the pressure of temptation was too strong, and that in a moment of sheer unconscious tumult of mind and heart the thing happened which was to wreck her youth.

On the special emotional circumstances of the war, it is impossible to improve upon the words of two politically active women who themselves lived through the war experience. Looking back from the 1930s, Mary Agnes Hamilton wrote sympathetically:

> Life was less than cheap: it was thrown away. The religious teaching that the body was the temple of the Holy Ghost could mean little or nothing to those who saw it mutilated and destroyed in millions by Christian nations engaged in war. All moral standards were held for a short moment and irretrievably lost. Little wonder that the old ideals of chastity and self-control in sex were, for many, also lost . . . The great destroyer of the old ideal of female chastity, as accepted by women themselves, was here. How and why refuse appeals, backed up by the hot beating of your own heart, or what at the moment you thought to be your heart, which were put with passion and even pathos by a hero here today, and gone tomorrow.[57]

Writing in 1916, Helena M. Swanwick was perhaps a shade less compassionate:

> The segregation of the sexes, which is one of the results of war, bringing with it, as it does, a peculiar enhancement of sexual appetite in men and a peculiar response in girls, makes for the growth of prostitution, but more immediately of promiscuity. Denied joy and tranquillity, men and women snatch at pleasure, gross and immediate. War-time brings its own devil-may-care state of mind in women as in men.[58]

For all the publicity that was given to war babies, it would be wrong to think that the war did much to mitigate the harsh conventions exacted by communities and families against the unmarried mother and her child. But at the level of authority and responsible social work, it did do something. Almost all of the leading women's organizations sponsored homes for war babies and their mothers; where women had to leave one of the auxiliary services or other Government employment because of pregnancy, the authorities at least tried to ensure that they were put in touch with one of the voluntary societies. This, of course, was still a very long way from the endowment of motherhood which feminists were calling for, and it did nothing, as Sylvia Pankhurst pointed out, to mitigate the miseries and misfortune which fell upon many girls of the poorer classes deserted by their soldier lovers.

The war, too, concentrated attention on the problems of what were called the 'Contagious Diseases'. It was a great tribute to governmental and administrative determination to break through the web of evasion and secrecy which enwrapped the subject before the war that in 1913 a Royal Commission on Venereal Diseases was established. The Battle of the Somme was at its height when the Commission published its final report, which, in calling for wider public knowledge and education and for 'a franker attitude towards these diseases' set the keynote for subsequent discussion, and to some extent chimed in with new informed attitudes which were developing anyway.

Much can be learned from the fascinating discussions on the day (6 July 1916) devoted to 'Sex Morality and Sex Education' at a conference held in London by the British Dominions Women's Suffrage Union.[59] A resolution against compulsory measures of legislation dealing with Venereal Disease was carried with four dissentients. As the mover of the resolution, Miss Alison Neilans, Editor of *The Shield*, and Assistant Secretary of the Association of Moral and Social Hygiene put it in her summing up: 'I cannot help believing that compulsory legislation will drive people to the sort of Quacks you see up and down Tottenham Court Road, "Specialists" for men and women.' Miss Maud Royden then moved: 'That while recognizing the value of the report of the Royal Commission on Venereal Disease, this Conference deplores the absence of any allusion to the low political and economic status of women and the intimate connection of this fact with Prostitution.'

Miss Royden began by arguing that while on the one hand there are 'women who appear, humanly speaking, to be naturally depraved', on the other hand, the vast majority of working women would not sell themselves at any price. She then went on to discuss what she called the confusion between immorality and prostitution. There were probably just about an equal number, proportionately, of naturally moral and immoral women in all classes; but when it came to prostitution, it was found that the very large majority came from the poorer classes.

I believe it is true that the number of women who are driven on the streets from fear of starvation is exceedingly small, but while we are perpetually being lectured about our gross materialism and reminded that man does not live by bread alone, I would suggest to such arguers that a woman may be starving of everything that makes life worth living long before she goes on the streets. (Applause) It is the grey and sordid monotony of the badly-paid girl, engaged in some unskilled, uninteresting, monotonous work, just at that age when romance and adventure and the first stirrings of sexual feeling make her demand from life colour and beauty and interest and love. That is often the real cause of the mischief. The fact that a girl will tell you when you ask her, how she came first into this life, that she sold herself for a silk blouse, or because she wanted to go to the theatre, surely ought to convey to anyone with any human sympathy that she sold herself because she must have some colour in her life, and because she cannot endure the sordid monotony of it. The more high-spirited, the more artistic, the more interesting she is, the less can she endure the absolutely monotonous greyness of sordid toil. Starvation does not begin with going without food, it ends there. (Applause)

Miss Royden then argued that it was a characteristic of modern industrial life that there were many women who led a 'straight life' as long as they could get employment, who then reverted to prostitution when unemployed. Many women 'pass only a few years living off and on the streets, and many of them afterwards marry or get into work on a firmer basis. Nevertheless, it is when the first barriers of self-respect are broken down, when a girl in that case of need does sell herself, that the downward path begins and the lowest class, the ultimate class of prostitutes, is largely recruited from these girls, who perhaps even for years were neither on the one side of the line nor the other, but always drifting in between.' It is, said Miss Royden, reverting to the main subject under discussion: 'the young girl, whom hardly anybody would have the heart to register as a licensed prostitute, who is the most actively infectious'.

The afternoon session on 'Sex Morality and Sex Education' is remarkable for showing the continued reticence and indeed prejudice of some of these bold and enlightened women. First of all, Norah March, BSc, author of *Towards Racial Health*, moved: 'That this Conference protests against the persistent ignoring of questions of sex in the moral and intellectual education of the young, and calls on all women's organizations to promote confidential and wholesome relations between parents and children and between teachers and children on this subject.'

In so doing, Miss March gave a somewhat obscure description of what she preferred to describe as the 'racial' organs. She was slightly more open on 'Sex Instinct' as an innate craving impelling organisms towards the performance of certain functions'. But the tone is idealistic:

In man, the sex instinct is different from what it is in animals, at least in some ways. It is different because it is more elaborate; essentially it is the same, but through the process of man's evolution, this instinct, which in animals is concerned with almost only a physical feeling, in man has become linked on to many of his more highly evolved activities. It has become linked on to filial affection, to comradeship, to the feelings of family life, to honour, to self-respect. We no longer speak of it as physical passion, but we call it love. That love is the mainspring of life, its biological destination is parenthood, and that is what we have to safeguard when we are contemplating sex education.

In strongly condemning fairy-tales about babies coming from cabbage patches or gooseberry bushes, Miss March was less than rigorous in the accuracy of her anatomical detail:

We have to recognize that children differ very much, and some children are satisfied with a very simple tale, but others want to know more. Some are satisfied that baby grew in a little nest in mother's body, just near her heart, but some say, 'But how did I get out?'

It is quite easy to say, 'Well, of course, nature made a little opening. Some children want to know where the opening is. 'Nature puts all her openings in places where no harm will come to them, and this opening from the nest is one of the most important openings of the body and therefore, placed in a very well protected part just between the hips.'

Father's role is quickly glossed over: it will be best be dealt with 'By having a simple study of plants and animals already in our minds, and having through that the right terminology to employ, the right explanation of the function may be given.'

It is perhaps worth pausing here to reflect that in recent years, anthropologists have given increasing attention to the images which women have of their own bodies. There can be little doubt that modesty and ignorance tended to go together in the Edwardian era; nor that the advent of internal tampons, oral contraceptives, and a general preoccupation with sexual functions, have contributed to the 'permissiveness' of today. In any case the growth of health education has been an important phenomenon which undoubtedly derived some impetus from the war. Mrs Drake from Sylvia Pankhurst's Workers' Suffrage Federation, did remark that 'These questions have been discussed in a very nice way', and then made the vital point that sex education was really needed among working-class women. She continued:

> To prove this I may mention the case of a policeman's wife whom I know. Her husband before their marriage had been a valet. He had not been brought up well. He had lived, and continued to live a 'fast' life. She was a country girl, a very good girl, whose only fault was absolute ignorance, the earliest result of which was the birth of the first child immediately after their marriage. The family number five now, and the two eldest are lovely girls of eleven and thirteen. The mother said to me, 'I must teach them: I cannot let them grow up and suffer as I did. I am afraid of their father's influence, and how can I safeguard them?' I advised her what simple books to get for her girls, and I realized then, as you must do, what a curse this conspiracy of silence is.

However, if this was a concealed plea on behalf of a diffusion of knowledge of contraception, Mrs Drake did not herself further break the silence on that point.

She was, in any case, immediately followed by the passionate Miss Abbadan, of the Catholic Women's Suffrage Society. The world, she said had become over-sexed: 'over-sexation has led to over-indulgence, over-indulgence has led to disease, disease has been carried by the man to his innocent wife and still more innocent child.' The truth of the matter was she declared, 'That it is the men who have taken the wheel of life, played with it like a naughty child, and broken it in pieces.' Miss Abbadan then went on to speak of what she called 'phallic worship'. 'It must be obvious, she continued with strong echoes of Emmeline Pankhurst's anti-male attitudes, 'that a man treats this particular function more as a sport than a woman does. He has no far-sighted expectancy of pain as a result of it He is the irresponsible pleasure-seeker; she is the responsible pain bearer.'

Finally, and perhaps predictably, Miss Abbadan launched into a peroration of Catholic puritanism:

We must reform the stage, we must purify fiction, we must fight drink, and we must reform dress. I welcome with all my heart the appearance of uniformed women. The less you differ from the man in dress, the less there will be of sex attraction. Help us to get rid of the doll, the parasite, for until they are gone you will not see woman as she was meant to be by her Maker.

Balance was restored in Miss March's summing up when she 'could not help feeling that the last speaker was rather hard on men'. But then her 'scientific' explanation, though fully in accordance with the assumptions of the time, and, no doubt, with the actual experience of most women of the time, left much to be desired as a final statement on the differences between men and women:

A man's physical organism is different from woman's, because the male organism has developed on a different line from the female organism. A woman has not only to perform a certain act as far as parenthood is concerned, but her body has to be prepared for nine months' nursing. We find that the woman's organism is less violent than the man's organism, because in man, the whole part that he has to play is one act only. Subsequently, the whole of his emotional condition is concentrated towards the performance of that act, and the sex feelings in man are consequently more violent than in women.

The whole answer was to: 'Help boys to grow up into men who will understand sex better, and who will be able to control themselves better.'

That the sexual feelings of men were more 'violent' than those of women continued to be the accepted wisdom, and therefore, for most women, the actual reality, until well after the Second World War. However, the First World War did mark the turning point in a process whereby it came to be regarded as normal and acceptable for women, as well as men, to acknowledge their sexual appetites. This is a crucial phenomenon in the emancipation of women.

Against that, one must put the undoubted fact that for the period under review, total, and as far as one can see, blissful, innocence continued to be the lot of a large number of unmarried girls. For all the officious prurience of the sanctimonious watchdogs, both female and male, we have many accounts of dances, walks, and other forms of fraternization between young men and young women which clearly, as far as the girls at least were concerned, were totally devoid of any thoughts at all of sex. There is a charming 'Diary of a Land Army Girl' written by a fourteen-year-old who raised her age to eighteen and enlisted in order to dodge domestic service. The Notts and Derby Regiment were stationed in the same village, and there was fierce competition among the soldiers to take the girls out for a stroll through the forest. But for this adolescent:

The one snag to this idyllic life was that I wouldn't fall in with these nocturnal wanderings. I wasn't in the least bit interested in boys, and at that time, had no idea what purpose they served. I remember vividly one evening. I had gone to the village, and saw two of the soldiers. They immediately offered to escort me home. This didn't suit me at all, as I wouldn't be able to sing my head off going through the forest, and for over two hours I argued with them, until eventually I told them that Robin Hood and his Merry Men would look after me. They gave me one startled look, saluted smartly, turned on their heels and made off as fast as their legs would carry them.[60]

'wo munitionettes at the Royal Arsenal, Woolwich. Note the wearing of slacks

When Mrs Gleason volunteered to go to Belgium with Dr Munro, Mairi Chisholm and the others, a main motive was that her husband was an American war correspondent already in Belgium. When the WAACS were established, it was an inflexible rule that no woman who had a husband serving in France or Belgium could enlist for service there. It was also a rule that no woman could get married within six months of enlisting. In her own scheme for a women's army corps Mrs Furse had reckoned that unmarried mothers, or those about to become so, would have to be discharged.

> They should not, however, be lost sight of, but their names and home addresses should be given to some competent organization with a view to their being properly cared for. As the responsibility for this will be for the men as well as the women, some definite action should be decided upon, and permitting marriage will be the only solution.

The authorities had all the other usual preoccupations as well: lectures on 'moral hygiene' were compulsory and there were all the rules about careful bounds and late passes, and so on.

Although there is little evidence of the seeking out of fugitive fathers, for almost the first year the not totally illiberal policy of granting pregnant women 'whether married or unmarried' sick leave without pay was followed. At the beginning of 1918, it was laid down that WAACS believed to be pregnant were to go before a medical board and if the pregnancy was confirmed they were to be discharged 'on medical grounds'. The same procedures were to be followed in regard to venereal diseases.

Members of the Women's Forestry Corps preparing food over an open fire. Note the breeches

Meantime, a new complication had arisen from the fact that a new order under the Defence of the Realm Act had made it a penal offence to communicate a venereal disease to a soldier. Almost immediately, soldiers in France began making charges against women of the WAAC: in one company seven such accusations were made, all of which were found to be untrue and three purely malicious.'

Unit administrators in the WAAC, were therefore asked:

> To give personal and confidential warnings to the women under their care of this risk, and to impress upon them the danger of going into lonely places, or in any way compromising themselves with unknown men, who may afterwards make entirely unfounded charges against them, and to point out the importance of keeping to main roads and frequented places when out with their soldier friends.[61]

Rumours of promiscuity among the WAACs became so virulent, that in February 1918, the Minister of Labour (G. H. Roberts of the Labour Party, it may be noted) appointed a Commission of Inquiry. Some measure of the advances made by the woman's cause can be found in the fact that all the Commissioners were women; two of them were women trade unionists. The Commission reported quite categorically that:

> We can find no justification of any kind for the vague accusations of immoral conduct on a large scale which have been circulated about the WAAC. The chief difficulty of our task has lain in the very vague nature of the damaging charges we were requested to investigate. It is common knowledge that fantastic tales have passed from mouth-to-mouth of the numbers of WAAC women returned to England for mis-conduct of the gravest character.[62]

WAACs bathing at
Paris-Plage, 29 May 1918

French, American and British soldiers with WAACS on Boulogne beach, 16 May 1918. Boulogne was the site of a transit camp

The Report then refuted these stories by citing the official statistics. On 12 March 1918, the WAAC strength in France was 6,023. By that time there had been 21 pregnancy cases (0.3 per cent of the total) and 12 venereal diseases cases (0.2 per cent of the total). Two of the pregnant women were married, and it appeared that the bulk of the others were pregnant before coming to France. With regard to the second category, several of the cases were apparently of old standing. In addition, nineteen women had been returned to England on disciplinary grounds and a further ten for inefficiency. In the period 1 July 1917 to 11 March 1918, there had been

Seventeen fines,
fourteen cases of confinement to camp,
twenty-three cases of restrictions of privileges,
seven admonitions,
a total of eighty-eight minor disciplinary actions.

The Commission then offered some discreet explanations of the origin of the rumours. 'It is generally admitted that a state of war tends in itself to create a somewhat abnormal and excited mentality, and that the general

126

atmosphere produced is one peculiarly favourable to the growth of fictitious tales.' Secondly, the Commissioners referred to the surprise of the French at the deportment of the WAACs: 'French customs and traditions of family decorum are far removed from the general social ideas which, in these latter times, regulate the intercourse of young men and young women of British origin.'

Letters home from British soldiers were also a source of rumours, partly because of the unworthy jealousy of men dislodged from non-combatant tasks, partly from the more worthy unwillingness to expose women to peril: 'In others, the element of sex jealousy in more than one form arises.'

The Report continued:

> Many officers, the Chaplains and also the officials of the YMCA, spoke with warm appreciation of the advantage to the soldiers of the possibility of frank and wholesome comradeship of women of their own race and the graver social dangers which such comradeship tended to avert. This point of view is confirmed by information given us in more than one sector to the effect that scandalous tales in connection with the WAAC had emanated from some of the low-class 'estaminets' (public houses), whose custom among British soldiers has suffered considerably owing to the better type of companionship now available for the men.

Psychologists have long noted that the need for immediate sexual release is very strong in men who have just come out of the fighting line. Very perceptively, the Commissioners referred to the special difficulties with regard to 'large numbers of uniformed young women' coming in contact with soldiers 'passing to and from the more electric atmosphere of the Line', and to the problems of 'the advanced posts where they are brought frequently into touch with men passing to and from the Line.' 'We are satisfied,' the Report said, 'that greater danger exists in these localities, than in the less emotional surroundings of the bases.'

Short Skirts and Painted Women

The press was full of articles on women's new jobs and women's new deportment. The *Daily Mail* had a piece in mid-September 1915 on 'Dining Out Girls':

> The wartime business girl is to be seen any night dining out alone or with a friend in the moderate-priced restaurants in London. Formerly she would never have had her evening meal in town unless in the company of a man friend. But now with money and without men she is more and more beginning to dine out.

The writer also noted the public smoking of 'the customary cigarette'.

Hints of the shortening of skirt-lengths as well as the occasional public smoking of cigarettes by *avant-garde* women, had appeared before the war. But the war itself was accompanied by more unusually rapid changes in women's fashions. The explanation that it was necessary for women engaged on war work to be unhampered by trailing skirts, may be psychologically perceptive, though in terms of dates, it is not strictly accurate. The first developments in fashion anticipated any wide use of women's desire to serve: the *Observer*'s Woman's Page talked of 'short full skirts' with 'more than a suspicion of ankle visible' in the first December of the war, of the 'extravagantly short skirt' at the beginning of January, and of 'skirts six inches off the ground' in February. Perhaps

EXHIBITION

of WAR ECONOMY DRESS.

MUST · BE · SEEN · BY · EVERYONE

Grafton Galleries, Bond Street.
10 to 6. From 3rd to 31st August (Inclusive)

1818

1918

The National Standard Dress will be demonstrated by
Mrs Allan Hawkey, The Inventor,
who will Lecture Daily.

MANY OTHER ATTRACTIONS

Orchestra will play daily.
Admission 1/3d Inclusive of Tax.

the crucial motivation was the desire to serve, combined with the shortage of luxury dress materials. The growth of women's employment certainly consolidated the new developments.

Lord Northcliffe, owner of the *Daily Mail*, became a powerful supporter of votes for women in the middle stages of the war. But his newspapers fought a bitter rearguard action against the new fashions; no doubt, in company with many of the older Suffragists and Suffragettes, he thought serious dedication to the National cause more important than any preoccupation with sexual attractiveness. 'Just now our young and pretty girls are pushing the craze for short skirts to the utmost limit', the *Daily Mail*, three months behind the times, declared in May 1915. 'But even now,' it tried to reassure itself, 'these ultra-remarkable models are regarded with suspicion by women of good taste.' A day or two later, it returned again to 'the walking skirt that is absurdly short' and which 'is not worn by the best-habited woman'. In June it was still pontificating about the 'extraordinarily short skirt . . . revealing, as it does, the feet and ankles and even more of the stockings'. But shorter skirts were not the whole of it. Girls engaged on farm-work took naturally to the wearing of trousers during their labours, and by an easy stage to the wearing of trousers even while off duty. The growth of the women's auxiliary organizations, with their 'trim short serviceable skirt' gave a further impetus to the shortening of skirt-lengths. *Punch*, as so often, summed it up neatly in a post-war cartoon in which a little girl looking at an Edwardian beauty asks, 'Mummy, hasn't she got any legs?'

The various instructions issued to women employed in different aspects of the national effort usually stressed the need to avoid cosmetics and indeed, the wearing of jewellery or any other adornment. In Victorian Britain there had been a reaction against the use of powders and rouges, whose use became associated with chorus girls, harlots and vamps. It is true that the foundations of the modern beauty trade were laid during the Edwardian period, but it took the stress and excitement of war, the affluence among the lower classes, and the greater spending money available to middle-class girls to bring a return to the heavy use of cosmetics. Towards the end of the war, the novelist Arnold Bennett noted in his diary, more as a piece of social reportage, than as a hostile criticism, the prevalence of 'painted women'. It was too readily assumed (mainly by men) that the new custom betokened 'sex absorption', but, as Mary Agnes Hamilton pointed out, it probably rather indicated 'self absorption'. Many women, for whom in pre-war days grinding work had made a mockery of any pretence at concern with personal appearance, were now beginning to take some pride in the way they looked. Small wonder if women performing long arduous tasks, covering long journeys in crowded trains and trams, facing the unremitting stares of their fellow human beings for whole days on end with scarcely the briefest interlude of privacy, felt the need for the bottles of powders, paints and creams offered by the cosmetics manufacturers. In view of today's fashions and attitudes, I leave it to someone else to determine the significance of the fact that it was during this war that the brassiere became a generally fashionable garment.

Whether imposed by society, or genuinely innate, a female characteristic apparent in the novels of Jane Austen and Charlotte Brontë, and long before and ever since, is a preoccupation with personal appearance. When Nurse F. E. Rendel, after incredible experiences, reached the Scottish Women's Hospital in Salonika in the last months of the war, she wrote to her mother:

Women's fashions from a poster

129

There were seventeen of us – 12 SWH [Scottish Women's Hospitals],
3 BRC [British Red Cross] and two army sisters. I am sorry to say
that four of the SWH people behaved disgracefully. They were very
noisy, flirted in the most brazen way, and were altogether obnoxious.
They weren't even pretty or young, but they were determined to be
surrounded by officers in spite of their ugliness and age and they
were successful.[63]

Good for them, one might say, despite Nurse Rendel's strictures! On
the home front it was presumably women who were behind the new
purchases of furs and pianos which were widely noted. Increasing expen-
diture on women's clothing was also noted, and was said to be generated
by women lower down the social scale than formerly.

A homely insight into what the ordinary factory worker might be
wearing, and what her ordinary life might be like, is given by the pamphlet,
*To Women War Workers: Some Homely Advice in Regard to the Mainten-
ance of their Health and Comfort*, Lilian A. Evans, Welfare Superintendent to St Helens' Cable and Rubber Company, Ltd.

CLOTHING . . . it it best to wear a woollen garment next to the skin,
but in those cases where wool irritates, a thin under-slip may be put
on first.

Never wear stiff, tight corsets. They induce dyspepsia and
digestive troubles of all kinds; they compress the ribs and internal
organs, and interfere with proper breathing. A soft, easy-fitting
corset that allows freedom of movement cannot do much harm.

Do not wear a lot of heavy skirts fastened round your waist, they
are injurious, costly and unnecessary, and sometimes dangerous.

On no account wear garters, either of elastic, tape, string, knitted
strips, or anything else. Stitch a piece of broad elastic to the bottom
edge of your corset at each side, and sew a button on the opposite
end. Fix a piece of tape as a corresponding loop on the top of your
stocking . . .

The basis of an ideal outfit for an indoor war-worker is as follows:–

A woollen combination, high-necked and short-sleeved, thick or
thin, according to the season of the year and the temperature of the
establishment where the work is performed. Soft, easy fitting corsets, with suspenders, as described above.

Cloth or tweed closed knickers, not too thick in texture, with
removable linings for washing each week. [In hot weather, or hot
factory conditions, sateen knickers could be worn].

A short garment of the Princess petticoat style, made of print or
sateen, may also be worn, though in Summer, or in a hot factory, a
thin camisole will be sufficient without an under-skirt.

The dress should be made in one piece, and should not reach
below the boot-tops, i.e., eight or ten inches from the ground. About
two and a half yards round the skirt edge is a convenient width . . .

Stockings should be of cashmere, or home-knitted ones. Semi-
transparent, artificial silk, or openwork stockings are an abomina-
tion in a factory or workshop . . .

BATHS. A fixed bath with hot and cold water, is not always to be
found in small houses . . . do not be discouraged. The whole body can
be washed in a bucket of warm water, using a piece of flannel and
mild soap . . .

ABOVE Women's football
team from Robinson's of
Chesterfield. Mrs Mosley
(née Layton) is second from
right bottom row, and her
friend Miss Florence Green,
third from right, was captain.
Robinson's developed the first
disposable sanitary towels in
the 1890s

Concert party organized by women carpenters near Calais to entertain wounded soldiers, 3 December 1918

BELOW WAACs and convalescent soldiers playing basket ball at WAACs camps, Etaples, 1 May 1918

bicycle: the encouraging of women to undertake physical exercise and free themselves from the heavy, unnatural clothing of an earlier era. *Bombshell*, described as the official organ of the National Projectile factory at Templeboro', in its issue for June 1917, gave reports of women's football games between D shop and A shop and D shop and Baker's Shell Factory. 'Who,' it asked, 'would have dreamed two years ago of women playing football?'

Whether through social conditioning or innate instinct, finding a husband was still a major objective of most young women. We get many glimpses of the war as the great matchmaker, bringing men and women together in situations which would have been unlikely in peacetime. Women were travelling more widely than ever before, learning a new confidence in themselves. But a horrible irony was that the war was also removing eligible young men from the home front, and, so often, destroying them. The shortage of men is a topic that we shall have to return to at the very end of this book.

Student flax workers drinking at a village pump on their way back to camp

Woman the Home-maker

The sharp price rises which we noted in the first stages of the war were followed by a brief plateau then by a further steady upward movement, so that in June 1915 food prices were about 32 per cent up on those of July, 1914. Butter was up by 2½d, bacon by 3d or 4d, cheese by 3d, pork sausages by 2½d and cooked meat by 4d to 6d (all per pound). If the standard working-class budget in 1914 is taken as 25 shillings and 8 pence per week, the equivalent figure was now 33 shillings or over. By September 1916 the increase (weighted by the Board of Trade in order to reflect actual spending habits) was 65 per cent. Price increases in towns with more than 50,000 inhabitants were noticeably greater (68 per cent) than those in small towns and villages (62 per cent). The highest increase of all was in the price of sugar, 163 per cent. Otherwise, increases were highest in the case of imported meat, as high as 123 per cent in the case of breast of mutton in town shops. Alternative sources of protein also rose steeply in price: fish, only up 70 per cent in country areas, was up 103 per cent in towns; eggs, on average, were up 82 per cent. A Government report of 1915 put the broad situation fairly:

Certain classes normally in regular employment, whose earnings have not risen in the same proportion as the cost of living – for example, the cotton operatives and certain class of day-wage workers and labourers – are hard-pressed by the rise in prices, and actually have to curtail their consumption even though the pressure of high prices may have been mitigated in some cases, by the employment of members of a family in munition work, and by the opening of better-paid occupations to women. Many people in receipt of small fixed incomes necessarily also feel the pressure; and it is obvious that while the total receipts of families past school age may have greatly increased, a family of the same class in which children are within school age may suffer exceptionally.

The weight of this exceptional burden inevitably fell on the housewife, who, while often having great difficulty in making ends meet, was at the same time exhorted by the Government to economize. The well-to-do, however, were exhorted not to economize too much since if they went for the cheaper items they would be depriving the poor of them. They were, moreover, asked to eat as little bread as possible, since it was quite openly recognized by the Government that bread was still the basic food item of the poor. The National Food Economy League published a series of guides, whose titles in themselves delineate the class structure:

Housekeeping on Twenty-Five Shillings a Week, or under, for a Family of Five
(priced at a penny);
Patriotic Food Economy for the Well-to-Do
(priced at sixpence);
War-time Recipes for Households where Servants are Employed
(also priced at sixpence).

One of the problems in regard to servants, apparently, was to stop them eating up the scraps of food which ought to have been re-incorporated in future meals. It is most instructive to set out side-by-side the menus advised for those housekeeping on 25 shillings a week, and those advised for the well-to-do. The former stated that breakfast should consist of porridge and milk for the children, eaten with a crust or toast (for the

We risk our lives to bring you food. It's up to you not to waste it.

J.P.Beadle.
1917

"A Message from our Seamen"

Food Economy Poster: 'We Risk Our Lives To Bring You Food'

teeth); and tea, bread or toast and margarine for the adults. Tea should consist of tea or cocoa, bread or toast and margarine or jam, and (every other day) scones (made of wholemeal or oatmeal), or oatcake or gingerbread. Daily menus were set out for the two main meals, dinner (in the middle of the day) and supper, which was for grown-ups only. Here are three sample menus:

[*First Day*]
DINNER
Scotch Barley Broth,
(one large sheep's head makes enough for two days)
Greens
SUPPER
Stewed Sheep's Tongue and Rice.

[*Fourth Day*]
DINNER
Meat Stew with Dumplings,
Potatoes,
Parsnips or Swedes,
Greens.
SUPPER
Lentil Soup with Toast.

[*Fifth Day*]
DINNER
Rice and Oatmeal Pudding
'*Dainty Pudding*'
SUPPER
Haricot Beans with Dripping

This may be contrasted with specimen menus for the well-to-do:

[*Monday*]
BREAKFAST
Egg Coquettes
(two eggs between six people)
Fried Sardines and Barley-Bread Croutes
Marmalade.
LUNCH
Oatmeal Mince
Puree of Cabbage
Jam Roly-Poly
(made with half barley, half wheat-flour)
DINNER
Palestine Soup
Chestnut Curry and Rice
Fruit Sago Shape.
Dessert.

[*Thursday*]
BREAKFAST
Fish Kedgeree
Marmalade
LUNCH
Chicken or Pheasant Braised with Vegetables
Steamed Oatmeal Gingerbread Pudding
Cheese and Biscuits

were supplied with materials for building shelters in the chalky slopes of their own gardens.

One of the most resented facets of war-time domestic economy was the rise in house rents. Women participated actively in the protest movement on Clydeside early in 1915, which led directly to the passing of the first Rent Restriction Act in British history. But bad housing, together with other grievances, contributed to the mood of extreme industrial unrest which characterized 1917. So much so, that on 13 June 1917, the Government appointed a series of Commissions of Inquiry into industrial unrest in eight separate areas of Great Britain. The reports were very fair in describing 'the hardship and actual privation' which many families were enduring but, typically enough, no one thought to interview housewives about their grievances. Still, progress was being made, and in the last year of the war the Ministry of Reconstruction, which recognized that a massive programme of state-subsidized housing would have to be undertaken, did go out of its way to try to secure the views of working-class women on what type of housing design they would favour. Less heartening was the fact that many of the working-class housewives interviewed were very hesitant over whether they had the right to ask for a fixed bath and, if so, whether it could be anywhere else than in the kitchen.

Austerity affected everyone, but as ever, some were more equal than others. For all the patriotic appeals, servant-keeping continued on a scale well-represented in wartime episodes of popular television series *Upstairs Downstairs*. Many wealthy women had never really had the problem of preparing the food for their families. However, from the very start of the war, middle- and upper-class women leapt into action in providing all sorts of canteens for soldiers and sailors: canteens in stations, in ports, in large towns and small, and also overseas in France, Belgium, and even Italy. Here is a contemporary account of the Free Church canteens for Soldiers and Sailors in Middlesbrough:

Inverness soldiers' and sailors' buffet

> The refreshment room in the Park was put at the disposal of a special committee by the lessee (Mr Dent), and, with the hearty cooperation of the Colonel, the Secretary organized a group of lady workers under the general management of Mrs Gaines, and every parade morning during a long and bitter winter supplied the men with a mug of hot coffee and a cake or biscuit. The officers of the battalion cordially assisted by so arranging the drilling of the Companies that in turn the men fell in for refreshments.
>
> The cost, which was heavy, was borne by voluntary subscriptions. Frequently over 1,000 men daily partook of the town's hospitality in this way.
>
> Both officers and men expressed the deepest gratitude and shared equally in the fare provided. the RSM said, 'I believe you have saved lots of these lads' lives'.
>
> Another branch of work largely organized by the Secretary was the securing of homes to which men were invited on Sunday afternoons and evenings. This spread through most of the churches and hundreds of men in this way found homes and friends which helped to make their stay in the town pleasanter and safer than it could otherwise have been. The troops at Maron Hall were included in this hospitality in the homes. Each Christmas and New Year the men were entertained to parties and suppers free of charge and many scores of concerts were given.[65]

Soldiers were not the only lonely people in Britain during the war;

ir wives, mothers, and sisters were often lonely too. Many of the men's organizations launched throughout the country provided ›ful support services for the troops, but their real function was provid-
; companionship for women themselves. The Imperial War Museum llection contains about twenty boxes of records of the various local ›anizations such as: the Bedworth 'Our Boys' Fund; the Bedwas and e-Thomas Red Cross Order of St John Sewing Guild; the Berwick-upon-›eed Army and Navy Recreation Room (whose members met every in passing throgh Berwick station); the Birdwell Patriotic Sewing mmittee; the Finchley War Hospital Supply Depot; the Inverness diers and Sailors Railway Station Canteen; the Kingswear Fund for awlers' Sea-boot Stockings for the Fleet; the Ollerton Soldiers' and ilors' Parcel Fund. The First Tipperary Rooms (named, of course, after t pre-war song which the first soldiers turned into the most popular and st nostalgic song of the war) for wives and relatives of sailors and diers were opened by Mrs Jason Kerr in Hammersmith, London, on October 1914. The Tipperary League was founded on 18 November 14, with clubrooms throughout the country. The motto of the League s 'Sister clasps the hand of Sister, Marching Onwards to the Light'. nong its most popular activities were: 'Afternoons for sewing, cutting t, singing, French home nursing, and talks on hygiene and mother-aft.'[66]

Women's Institutes had existed in Canada, and subsequently in the iited States, since the late nineteenth century. Mrs Alfred Watt (adge Robertson), the Canadian wife of Alfred Tennyson Watt of the ›minion Civil Service, British Columbia, and daughter of Henry ›bertson, KC, of Strewan, Collingwood, Ontario, introduced the idea :o Britain. Despite official discouragement, Mrs Watt got the move-ent going, and eventually, in October 1917, the Board of Agriculture ›k over its sponsorship. The Institutes again combined the function of ›viding meeting places for women, and of carrying on such war work the collection of valuable waste materials and the provision of gifts r the troops. Like the Tipperary Rooms, and other similar organizations, ey too contributed to that raising of consciousness which was the most ›portant legacy of the First World War to British women.

ildren and Welfare

ie dislocations of war intensified women's responsibilities and fficulties in regard to the upbringing of their children. In 1915 the ·cretary of the Howard Association of London, Cecil Leeson, reported untly that war conditions were intensifying juvenile delinquency d disrupting family life. In the long term the war did bring desirable ucational reform, but in the short term it brought intense pressure ›on local authorities to suspend the school attendance by-laws. ›unty magistrates were especially anxious that children should be leased to undertake 'National work' (that is to say work on the farms the county magistrates). A sad letter from the Secretary of one County lucation Committee to the Board of Education explained the import-ice of paying heed to 'influential persons, including magistrates, airmen of district councils, and so on' and the danger of alienating the ympathies of magistrates and employers of labour.'[67] More humane otives played a part too. Some families were placed in a serious plight hen the one wage-earner was on active service overseas; pleas for the lease of school children based on straitened family circumstances were t easy to resist. Thus in August 1917, H. A. L. Fisher, President of the

Board of Education, admitted in the House of Commons that during the first three years of war 600,000 children had been put 'prematurely' to work; this figure did not include the hundreds of other children set to work in total violation of the law. The final report of the 1917 Departmental Committee on Juvenile Education was extremely gloomy:

> Parental control, so far as it formerly existed, has been relaxed, largely through the absence of families from their homes . . . Even the ordinary discipline of the workshop has in varying degrees given way; while the withdrawal of influences making for the social improvement of boys and girls has in many districts been followed by a noticeable deterioration in behaviour and morality. Gambling has increased. Excessive hours of strenuous labour have over-taxed the powers of young people; while many have taken advantage of the extraordinary demands for juvenile labour to change even more rapidly than usual from one blind alley employment to another.

That was one by-product of the recruitment of husbands and fathers into the armies, and of women and mothers into the factories. But another was the development of what the Chief Inspector of Factories and Workshops described as 'a striking degree of solicitude on the part of the managers for [the women's] welfare and comfort'. Welfare facilities were by no means completely lacking in British factories before the war. An enthusiastic young research student from Australia, drawing her evidence from the last year of peace and the first year of war, before the influx of women had had time to make itself felt, was able to compile a 300 page tome on British welfare work. In a preface to the book, which was published in 1916, when the topic was becoming one of pressing interest, Lloyd George stressed that great and important changes had taken place since the completion of the text; in particular the modest private initiatives in the matter had been bolstered by the inception of a special Welfare Department at the Ministry of Munitions.[68]

Before the war, Factory Inspectors had for many years been pressing upon employers the advisability of the provision of qualified medical services, of the setting aside of canteens and restaurants, of the supervision of women factory workers by women welfare officers, and of the need for hygienic lavatory and washroom facilities, especially where there were employees of both sexes in the same workshop. It was on the last point that complaints were most prevalent. The Lady Inspector for the North West reported in 1913:

> It is impossible to describe in a public paper how low the standard had been and still is in many places, where in other respects the conditions are not only not noticeably bad, but are quite good.

In 1915, great advances in welfare work were noted, with arrangements for dealing with sickness and injury appearing, as well as canteen and messrooms. The reasons were various. The employment of women where no women had been employed before, and the employment especially of the delicate flower of the middle and upper classes, was definitely the starting-point at the personal level of individual employer-employee relationships, though its importance must not be over-stressed. Britain had a long tradition of factory acts designed to protect women and children, but qualified by the persisting belief that to attempt to legislate for the adult male was to reflect upon his manhood.

The hectic conditions of the Home Front created new needs. The concentration of labour in a munitions centre brought a heavy pressure

ABOVE Canteen at Woolwich Arsenal

RIGHT Munitions welfare: attending a light casualty in the hospital of a shell-filling factory

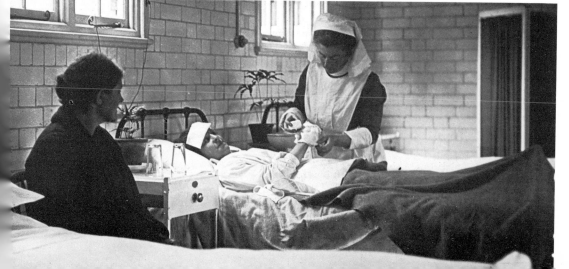

on available accommodation, so that it became not unusual for the same bed to be in use day and night, first for a night-shift worker, then for a day-shift worker. In other cases, the worker, man or woman, might have long distances to travel each day, which, when added to the over-time hours frequently worked, might leave barely six hours available for sleep. Attention was therefore directed to problems of fatigue, sickness and nutrition; in the case of girls living, or daily travelling, far from home, there was felt to be an especially strong case for the establishment of welfare supervisors. For women working on TNT, a free daily pint of milk was provided.

Some innovations were less well received than others by the factory workers. Canteens, in time of food difficulty, performed a welcome task

Interior of the Princess
Victoria Rest Club for Nurses,
Etaples, 7 November 1917
INSET WAACS in their
dormitory at Rouen,
24 July 1917

1 providing cheap, if not exciting, food. A typical menu ran: 'Sausage
nd Mash, 2½d; Mince and Mash, 2d; Patties, 1d; Beans, 1d; Stewed Fruit,
l; Milk Pudding, 1d'. But rebellious working-class spirits and indepen-
ent-minded women were frequently resentful of welfare supervision,
^hich, with shrewd cynicism, they saw as merely a paternalistic attempt
o maintain their efficiency as so many units of labour in the total sum of
roduction. Nevertheless, when the Chief Factory Inspector, in his
eport for 1915, suggested that the war-time welfare schemes would be
ikely to be felt and to spread long after the war has ended, and to leave
ehind a permanent improvement in factory life', he was making an
minently sound prediction which subsequent industrial history more
1an vindicated.

American nurses arriving at Brest, 5 May 1918

CHAPTER SIX

WOMEN'S RIGHTS

1916–1919

Discrimination

The disabilities under which women laboured can be broadly defined as economic, social and sexual, and political, though in practice they overlapped and reinforced each other. In some cases, voting rights and matrimonial matters, for instance, there was a clear issue of law. In other cases it was often simply a matter of social custom and convention. Many cases, as the war experience sometimes revealed, were a mixture of both. Law and custom, prejudice and misconception, had become woven together into an almost seamless web by which women were hampered, but from which, due to the exceptional circumstances of the war they were now sometimes able to escape. At times there were arguments as to just where the escape lay. Many men, and some women, argued that some laws, such as those affecting factory welfare or divorce, were designed to protect the interests of women themselves. One wretched symptom of the state of law and opinion was the frequency of 'breach of promise' proceedings. Divorce was an issue on which feminists were divided. Editorially, *Votes for Women* was in favour of divorce by consent after three years, but many readers wrote in to say that this would be very much to the disadvantage of women. Here the factor of differential aging was significant: even in 1969 Dr Edith Summerskill was to refer to the Divorce Reform Act of that year as a 'Casanova's Charter'. At a further biennial Conference in 1918, the Dominions Women's Suffrage Union did discuss divorce, but did not pass any resolutions or take any votes. That crucial woman's right, as many would see it today, access to, and knowledge of, contraception, was again never once mentioned.

Openly or covertly, women were handicapped in the achievement of status and promotion. The war threw up a fascinating range of examples. Two of the great war heroines were the distinguished surgeons Dr Flora Murray and Dr Elizabeth Garrett Anderson, who returned from France to run the Women's Hospital Corps Military Hospital at Endell Street in London. As doctor in charge, Dr Murray, in theory, had the status of a woman Lieutenant-Colonel in the British Army. But, in fact, as a fellow feminist commented: 'The War office withheld from her both the title and the outward and visible signs of authority.' The same woman writer continued, in a manner to be echoed up and down the country, that if Dr Murray and Dr Garrett Anderson had:

> failed to satisfy the Authorities even in the slightest detail, there is not much doubt but that the charge of the Hospital would have been handed over to a man, and that more than one military official would have had the joy and triumph of saying:
> *'There* – I told you so. The women have failed medically and administratively, and have been unable to maintain discipline.'[69]

It may be noted that Dr Murray refused to participate in the collection of materials in regard to women's war work by the Imperial War Museum, because she wished her hospital to be considered purely professionally as a military hospital and not as women's war work.

No other country in the world followed Britain in enrolling women in the highly sensitive work of the Postal Censorship. The women were said to have worked effectively and with discretion, but no woman came anywhere near any of the senior posts within the Postal Censorship.[70] The story could be repeated hundreds of times. Much was made of the fact that in the factories and on the farms it was usually calculated that it would need three women to do the work of two men. Much less was made of the fact that 5 VAD women could replace 8 men[71] – though admittedly in the sort of work traditionally regarded as being women's anyway.

The status of the married woman was a headache in many sorts of ways. At one stage there was a worry within the WAAC organization that a woman who had enrolled as a single person, but then got married, might now fall under her husband's jurisdiction. However, the ruling was obtained that the woman could be made to 'continue on exactly the same conditions that she would have done had she not married after signing on with the Women's Army Auxiliary Corps'.[72] It does have to be said that the actual enrolment form for the WAAC nowhere requested any indication of a husband's approval; the one restriction, it will be recalled, was that a married woman was not allowed to serve in France if her husband was already there. The conventional wisdom of the time, despite the conspicuous example of Mary Macarthur, wife of the Labour MP W. C. Anderson, was that a successful career for a woman was not compatible with marriage. At the end of 1917, Vaughan Nash, Permanent Secretary at the Ministry of Reconstruction, conducted a correspondence with the Heads of Oxford and Cambridge Ladies' Colleges and unabashedly filed them under the heading 'wastage due to marriage'. The information he was requesting was the number of women from each College who had taken a degree or its equivalent and who had married during the twenty years before the outbreak of war, having before marriage definitely engaged in paid professional work, and the age at which they did get married. In their replies, most of the Heads of the Ladies' Colleges pointed out that a number of women had continued to work after marriage, a point which Vaughan Nash had ignored in his original letter and continued to ignore thereafter.[73]

Feminists had long argued that the courts frequently applied unequal standards against females as compared with males, particularly in matters of a sexual nature. Votes for Women, the organ of the United Suffragists, continued into the war its series on 'Comparison of Punishments' where legal verdicts were set out side-by-side in order to point up the contrast. At the Imperial Woman's Suffrage Conference of 1916, Miss Evelyn Sharp spoke to the resolution that 'Inequalities of administration of law in cases of sexual crime be thoroughly ventilated at public meetings and in the press.' She accused magistrates and judges of eagerness to acquit men accused of assaulting girls under the age of consent, if their defence was that they thought the girl was actually over sixteen. Even where judges took a stricter view, the all-male juries, she argued, would side with the defendant. Not all of the accusations against the courts seem to me to be fully sustainable, if only because the rights and wrongs of such cases are often particularly difficult to determine. In August 1917, Votes for Women reported exuberantly that:

No humane person will feel anything but intense relief at the acquital of Miss Alice Roberts, the domestic servant of sixteen who was charged at Glamorgan Assizes on 20 July with the murder of a farm servant. The reason alleged for her action was that he had tried to assault her improperly on more than one occasion.

But there could be no quibbling with Evelyn Sharp when she stated that the only real solution would be to have women magistrates, women solicitors, women barristers, women judges and women on juries.

The vast majority of women who took up new types of employment during the war, whether as WAACs or tram conductresses, munitionettes or land workers, were in no way consciously working for women's rights. Yet, just by doing new jobs, and doing them well, they achieved much. The Suffragettes, in the early stages of the war, played an important part in encouraging women to push themselves forward for all sorts of jobs. Above all, the Women's Interests Committee of the NUWSS played a key role in agitating on behalf of both job opportunity and equal pay. This Committee pressed the Government on the pay rates of women in the higher Civil Service, and on the need to employ women in Government Committees. It pressured the Post Office into providing suitable conditions for postwomen; and it succeeded in persuading employers to employ women rather than the boy labour which many originally preferred.[74] Government policy, especially through the Ministry of Munitions, as we have seen, also helped to ensure that reasonable pay levels were introduced for women.

However, although the gains were real and many, the forces resistant to any universal concept of equal pay for equal work are clearly apparent in the last year of the war. In 1918, the War Cabinet set up a special committee on Women in Industry, under the Chairmanship of the Hon. Mr Justice Atkis, which finally reported in 1919. Highly significantly, there was a special Physiological Sub-Committee. On it were Dr Janet Campbell and the redoubtable Beatrice Webb; but for anyone who knows anything about the working of committees, it is obvious where the power lay – with Lieutenant-Colonel the Right Honourable Sir Mathew Nathan, who doubled as Chairman and Secretary and who was also Secretary to the parent Committee. But anyway not all the women interviewed were helpful to the woman's cause. The woman Medical Officer of the National Filling Factory at Aintree declared that 'there is more hysteria in the women' and then added unsympathetically that 'we cure them by telling them that if they have another hysterical attack they have to leave'. Throughout the shorthand transcriptions of the evidence, both Atkis and Nathan show a clear inclination towards believing in the innate disabilities of women. Atkis in interviewing Mrs Corbett Ashley made a point which has been repeated over and over again right up to our own day, asking whether in assuming all the rights of men, women would also take on all the duties of men. Mrs Corbett Ashley seemed inclined to agree that women did have some natural disability which, she said, 'would have its full weight, but not more than its full weight'. She was willing to accept the Chairman's formulation of, not equal pay for equal work, but equal pay for equally efficient work.[75]

On the Sub-Committee, Nathan put to Miss Constance Smith, HM Senior Lady Inspector of Factories, North-Eastern Division, a leading question: did she believe that equal pay would tend to exclude women from jobs which they might otherwise reasonably get? But Miss Smith was not be browbeaten, and gave a categorical negative. She then proceeded to develop the argument that although equal pay might result immediately in some women losing their jobs, it could only be beneficial in its long-term effects since it would encourage women to train properly for the better jobs. Miss Smith came out firmly in favour of equal pay for the same work rather than equal pay for equal productive value. This was faithfully recorded in the printed version of her evidence made available to Parliament and the public, but in condensing the rest of her argument it was subtly mis-represented so that the main weight was given to the statement that equal pay 'would very likely result in displacing a certain number of women from industry'.[76] This subtle misrepresenting of the evidence of women factory inspectors and Civil Servants, who really did know what they were talking about, in order to conform with prevailing prejudices about equal pay is to be found on several occasions. Compare, for example, the actual shorthand transcription of two key sentences of Miss A. M. Anderson in her evidence to the Sub-Committee, with the published version. Miss Anderson actually said:

> The artificial and conventional crowding of women into concentrated areas has been disastrous economically to them and lessened their power in every way to secure by bargaining, conditions physiologically and otherwise suitable to them. It is a fallacy to assume that because women may need for their best work conditions and methods of working different from those hitherto prevailing for men to a large extent, they will in the long run be economically less advantageous to employ.[77]

This becomes:

> The concentration of women in a limited number of trades has been disastrous to them economically. Because women need for their best work conditions and methods of work not hitherto used in men's employment, it does not follow at all necessarily that they are less economically advantageous to employ.[78]

The possibility that women may need special conditions has become a definite statement that they do need special conditions while Miss Anderson's categorical statement that it is a fallacy to think women economically less advantageous to employ has now become the much more equivocal statement that this 'does not follow at all necessarily'. Thus men rewrite history to suit themselves.

Votes for Women

The issue which, after decades of Suffragist and then Suffragette agitation, and eighteen months of bloody total war, brought votes for women back into the forefront of practical politics was that of votes for men. Because votes for men were based on the antiquated residential qualification, thousands of men had actually lost their right to vote through going out to serve their country. Thousands of other men who were also serving their country had never had the vote in the first place. Consideration of these problems, inevitably brought the question of votes for women into full view. All this is not to say that the various suffrage societies had shut up shop as historians sometimes maintain. The United Suffragists and the Women's Freedom League were still very active; the National Union of Women's Suffrage Societies had seized the opportunity provided by the war to concentrate on social and economic rather than political matters, but it was prepared to resume agitation

'Votes For Heroines As Well As Heroes': cartoon from 'Votes For Women' 26 November 1915

just as soon as the war ended. Still it is inescapably true that war-time conditions simply were not suitable for open demonstrations; and also that few of the women really believed that there was any likelihood of a Suffrage Act being passed in time of war.

Rumours about possible changes in the franchise for men began to circulate in late 1915. In January 1916, a number of the suffrage organizations held a private meeting in London which, while showing that there wàs still strong differences of opinion between those who favoured complete adult suffrage, and those who simply wanted women to be enfranchised on the same terms as men, did produce an agreed resolution that any bill increasing the number of voters should be so framed as to include the enfranchisement of women.[79] In May, Mrs Fawcett raised the issue directly in a letter to Asquith:

When the Government deals with the franchise, an opportunity will present itself of dealing with it on wider lines than by the simple removal of what may be called the accidental disqualification of a large body of the best men in the Country, and we trust that you may include in your Bill clauses which would remove the disability under which women now labour. An agreed Bill on these lines would, we are confident, receive a very wide measure of support throughout the Country. Our movement has received very great accessions of strength during recent months, former opponents now declaring themselves on our side, or at any rate, withdrawing their opposition. The change of tone in the Press is most marked . . . The view has been widely expressed in a great variety of organs of public opinion that the continued exclusion of women from representation will . . . be an impossibility after the war.[80]

Asquith denied that alteration of the Register was being contemplated, but added that if such an alteration should become necessary Mrs Fawcett's points would be 'fully and impartially weighed without any prejudgment from the controversies of the past'.

From inside Government itself, the officials of the Local Government Board placed before the Cabinet the argument in favour of a comprehensive bill simplifying the existing system of franchise and registration, and the Labour Cabinet Minister, Arthur Henderson, put forward a paper calling for universal adult suffrage.[81] However, Henderson wanted the qualifying age for women to be 25, not 21, as for men: this is an important point – even democrats feared seeing women in an overall majority in the country, particularly since they were widely believed to be a conservative force. Questions in the House of Commons about the Government's intentions brought the matter back into the headlines and roused the NUWSS to action; a joint Suffrage Conference in June agreed that if an extension of the male franchise was intended then agitation for female suffrage must be resumed. NUWSS deputations were received by Asquith on 25 July, and by Bonar Law and Lord Robert Cecil, a strong Tory supporter of the women's cause within the Cabinet, on 3 August. The main points made by the women, set out in another letter to Asquith on 4 August, were that, provided there were no proposals to alter the basis of the old Register (as opposed to the modifications necessary to enable voters who had enlisted to maintain their qualification) they would not resume their agitation: they would, however, force the suffrage issue if the male vote was to be extended, or if it were intended to hold a General Election. It was at this point that Mrs Pankhurst signalled her effective abandonment of the suffrage fight by letting it be known that she was in

favour of soldiers and sailors getting the vote whether or not women got it as well.

The Government introduced its Special Register Bill in Parliament on 14 August, but there were so many other issues, apart from votes for women, including the question of plural voting and the possible introduction of proportional representation that it was finally decided that all of these problems should be referred to a committee representing all parties and drawn from both houses of Parliament, to sit under the chairmanship of the Speaker.

The deliberations of the Speaker's Conference, which held its first meeting on 12 October, were secret, and it refused to hear evidence from the NUWSS. The Speaker, J. W. Lowther, cleverly got all the other contentious issues settled, before turning to that of women's suffrage. A majority of fifteen to six favoured at least some votes for some women; by twelve votes to ten it was agreed that there must be some restriction to prevent women voters from being in the majority.[82]

The advent of the Lloyd George Government in December 1916 augured well for the women. The press magnate, Lord Northcliffe, was a supporter of the women's case, as well as of Lloyd George, and he was able to drum up some favourable publicity in his newspapers. Reporting on 30 January 1917, the Speaker's Conference unanimously supported three basic propositions and a host of lesser ones. The three proposals were that the unsatisfactory occupational basis of the existing franchise should be replaced by a simple residential qualification (this was soon carried out), that there should be a simplification of the Local Government Register (this was also carried out), and that proportional representation should be introduced (this was never carried out, showing that recommendations of the Conference were not necessarily bound to be accepted by Parliament). Unanimity, anyway, was lacking on Section Eight of the report, the one which dealt with women's suffrage. It read as follows:

Funeral of a nursing sister killed during the bombing of the hospital at Etaples, 3 June 1918

The conference decided by a majority that some measure of woman's suffrage should be conferred. A majority of the Conference was also of the opinion that, if Parliament should decide to accept the principle, the most practical form would be to confer the vote in the terms of the following resolution:

'Any woman on the Local Government Register who has attained a specified age, and the wife of any man who is on that register, if she has attained that age, shall be entitled to be registered and to vote as a Parliamentary elector.'

or the 'specified age' the report suggested 30 or 35. Apart from this projected age-bar, there was an implied property and class qualification: ly householders were on the Local Government Register. In the country large there were over 12,000,000 women aged 21 or over: under 9,000,000 eld the necessary household qualification, and an age-bar of 30 would duce that number to under 7,000,000.

To keep up the pressure on the Government, and to affirm that there ad been no slackening in women's support for the principle of votes r women the London Society for Women's Suffrage organized a Women Workers' Suffrage Demonstration' at the Queen's Hall on) February. It was left to the Executive and then the National Council the NUWSS, to grasp the problem of the unequal treatment for men and omen proposed by the Speaker's Conference. Again under Mrs Fawcett's rewd leadership, the National Council endorsed the Executive's solution that the NUWSS should for the moment drop its older demands r complete equality and go hard for a bill along the lines recommended the Speaker's Conference. This caused enormous heart-searching ithin the suffrage movement so that a special circular letter had to be nt out explaining that Mrs Fawcett and Mrs Strachey had interviewed vo members of the War Council and seven members of the Government efore concluding that it was vital to support a compromise measure. In articular, Mrs Fawcett and Mrs Strachey had been informed: 'That no ll of any sort will be introduced unless the Government feels assured

Inspecting women police outside their barracks at Gretna

that there will be practical unanimity in the House and little opposition in the country, the Government preferring an immediate General Election on the old Register to wasting time over controversy in the House of Commons.' Furthermore, moderate anti-suffragists were prepared to accept this as a working compromise for the sake of clearing the decks for home legislation after the war. On the other hand, argued Mrs Fawcett and Mrs Strachey, supporters of complete adult suffrage accepted it as an instalment for the sake of breaking down the sex barrier, and because it would lead to a further extension in the near future.[83]

The next development in Parliament was a highly significant one. Asquith, ousted Prime Minister, bastion of the resistance to the women's claims in pre-war days, reluctant conceder of women's value in time of war, now moved a resolution calling for an early bill to implement the recommendations of the Speaker's Conference. 'Some of my friends may think,' he said contritely, 'that . . . my eyes, which for years in this matter have been clouded by fallacies and sealed by illusions, at last have been opened to the truth.' The motion was passed by 341 votes to 62.

The next day, Saturday 29 March, came the very cheerful occasion of the women's suffrage deputation received by Lloyd George at 10 Downing Street. It was an imperial as much as a national occasion; but there were no Duchesses, and the working-class woman at least got a mention if not exactly a look-in. After Mrs Fawcett had explained their willingness to support an imperfect scheme, the next speaker was HM Chief Lady Factory Inspector, the Miss Anderson we have met already. She introduced herself as a 'daughter of Greater Britain'. She had been born in Australia, and had had links of every kind with Australia and New Zealand, 'the homes of enfranchised women'. She concluded with some words on the British working woman:

> The last thing I want to do is to make her out a paragon which she is not; but I do maintain that the least thing we have to fear is danger to our Country if the English, Scottish, and Irish women should ever voice their own political, industrial, and social needs, which are those of their fathers and husbands, and lovers and brothers, and children also. Anyone who has a thinking mind knows and admits that these women are worthy of better conditions than they have, whether in their dwellings, or their occupations, or their wages. The first step – the urgent step – is to consult them; and the next thing, it seems to me, is to go on consulting them.

The emphasis on women workers was continued through the introduction of the next speaker, Mary Macarthur. The imperial theme was continued by Mrs Watt, of Canada, whose brief it was to 'draw attention to some of the imperial aspects of the suffrage question'. Then, at the special request of the Prime Minister, Mrs Pankhurst spoke, but more in the interests of compromise than of women's suffrage:

> I want to say for members of my organization; and I think for patriotic women generally, that we recognize that in war-time we cannot ask for perfection in any legislation; and although in times of peace we should want to debate every item of a Bill – we should want to discuss every part of it – in war-time we want to see this thing done as quickly as possible, with as little dispute and as little difference of opinion as possible. And so we ask you, Mr Lloyd George, to give such a Government measure to the House of Commons to vote upon as you feel to be just and practicable in the

war circumstances; and I want to assure you that whatever you think can be passed, and can be passed without discussion and debate as possible, we are ready to accept. (Here, here) We know your democratic feeling, and we leave the matter in your hands. We only ask you to make yourself, as Prime Minister responsible for it, and to give you great influence and great energy for carrying it through as quickly as possible.

Lloyd George followed with a long speech of his own. He admitted that an age-bar was 'illogical and unjustifiable'. But, he said, the compromise measure would no doubt lead later to equal rights. At this point, a member of the Workers' Suffrage Federation chipped in to support votes for women under 30. Lloyd George's curt reply was that he had nothing more to say; he had already explained the position. On that cue, Mrs Fawcett hastily brought proceedings to a close.

The Government's Bill, which settled upon 30 as the minimum voting age for women and gave the vote to all adult males passed through the House of Commons fairly easily in June 1917: the largest vote against the women's suffrage clause was 55. The House of Lords, which still had the power to delay legislation, might have been a tougher proposition. The debate in the upper chamber took place on 11 January 1918: Lord Curzon spoke against votes for women, but recommended abstention in order to avoid a clash with the House of Commons. In fact, the bill secured a very convincing majority of 136 to 71, and it passed into law on 6 February 1918.

Martin Pugh has argued that it was a muted victory, and less than the women would have got had there been no war. With this I cannot agree. The most clear-sighted supporters of women's suffrage recognized it for the tremendous victory that it was. The United Suffragists reckoned it a vital, and irresistible stage towards complete women's suffrage, and indeed brought publication of their journal *Votes for Women* to an end.

The Crumbling Fortresses of Prejudice

To say that the war brought votes for women is to make a very crude generalization, yet one which contains essential truth. To understand it fully, one must see the question of women's rights not in isolation, but as part of a wider context of social relationships and political change. It is perfectly true that a broad, liberal-democratic movement starting in the late nineteenth century had come near to achieving votes for women before 1914; it had certainly made many other achievements. Yet the political advance of women in 1914 was still blocked by two great fortresses of prejudice: the vigorous hostility of men, and the often fearful reluctance and opposition of many women. The many developments we have discussed in this book brought a new confidence to women, dissipated apathy, silenced the female anti-suffragists. Asquith was only the most prominent of the converts among men. No doubt the actual swing-round among members of the House of Commons was not enormous; certainly as politicians, whatever their private convictions, most felt that it was no longer politically wise to oppose women's suffrage tooth and nail. No doubt many agreed with a member of the Conservative Party Central Office that: 'the granting of a vote to the wives of duly qualified male electors would as a rule increase the majority of the opinions of the male voters.'[84] Undoubtedly the replacement of militant suffragette activity by frantic patriotic endeavour played its part as well.

More than this, the war generated a tremendous mood favourable to change and democratic innovations. An editorial comment on Mrs

Pankhurst's first great recruiting speech had hinted at this as early as November 1914: 'After this war many things can never again be as they were before it broke out. Some of the changes, perhaps, may be for the worse; the majority . . . will, we trust, be for the better. Is it too much to hope that the altered position and prospects of the women's movement will be among the national gains?' Such sentiments were repeated over and over again till some people actually begun to believe in them. From May 1915 there were Labour members in the Government, and although they wanted many other things, no doubt more pressingly, they also supported votes for women. Whatever might or might not have happened had there been no war, only the war could have provided the concentrated experience which both gave to women a new confidence in themselves, and showed up the absurdities of the many preconceptions about what they were capable of. The words of politicians are not usually the most reliable of historical sources. But E. S. Montague, Lloyd George's successor as Minister of Munitions, put the matter well when on 15 August 1916 he said in Parliament: 'Women of every station . . . have proved themselves able to undertake work that before the war was regarded as solely the province of men.' The armies had been saved, and victory had been assured, by women. 'Where,' he asked, 'is the man now who would deny to women the civil rights which she has earned by her hard work?'

The wspu, in November 1917, became the Woman's Party, under the leadership of Christabel Pankhurst. It preached a kind of national socialism, care for the poor and weak, but hostility to trade unions, and glorification of what Christabel called 'Captaincy' in industry.

Christabel's, and the country's main enemy was still Germany. But in June 1918, another enemy arrived on the scene, picking off women and children as well as men, impartial in its attacks on all social classes. The first wave of the great influenza epidemic reached its peak in the second week of July, shortly followed by a second wave which came to its high-point in the first week of November. The final wave appeared towards the end of January 1919, and reached its crest in the last week of February. Total deaths were 151,446 (140,989 civilians), between a fifth and a quarter of total deaths from military action.

But at last the war news was good. No doubt few ordinary housewives shared in the sense of excitement and colour which began to return to the big cities. Some, no doubt, attempted to forget their war weariness in following the amazing trial at the old Bailey, in which Pemberton Billing, MP, was prosecuted for libelling a dancer, Maud Allan, as a sexual pervert. The defendant secured acquittal and public acclaim by alleging the existence of a 'black book', compiled over 20 years by German agents, and containing the names of many prominent British men and women, with a catalogue of their sexual weaknesses.

While the press, in October, began to talk of the imminent collapse of the Germans, the bill completing the political emancipation of women was rushed through Parliament. Its single important clause read:

A woman shall not be disqualified by sex or marriage for being
elected to, or sitting or voting as a Member of the Commons House
of Parliament.

LEFT Officers of the Queen Mary's Army Auxiliary Corps working under the DPM at Cologne in the permit office, dealing with requests to pass out of the occupied zone, early 1919
BELOW Electioneering on behalf of Christabel Pankhurst

CHAPTER SEVEN

'THE GREAT SEARCHLIGHT OF WAR'

The firing of maroons had been used as an air-raid-warning signal, the last having been heard in May. Then once more, at 11 a.m. on 11 November 1918, the maroons boomed again. Michael McDonagh, the London journalist, 'rushed out and inquired what was the matter. "The Armistice" they exclaimed, "The War is Over!"' With greater sensitivity than most people were able to show at the time, he continued in his diary:

> I sorrowed for the millions of young men who had lost their lives; and perhaps more so for the living than for the dead – for the bereaved mothers and wives whose re-awakened grief must in this hour of triumph be unbearably poignant.

Crowd outside Buckingham Palace on Armistice Day, 11 November 1918

Vera Brittain, a middle-class girl who had made it to Oxford just when the war broke out, and had served as a VAD, both in France and now again back in London, had just resolved she must marry her sweetheart Roland, before it was too late, when in 1915, news came of his death at the Front. She was at her hospital on Millbank when she:

heard the maroons crash with terrifying clearness, and, like a sleeper who is determined to go on dreaming after being told to wake up, I went on automatically washing the dressing bowls in the annex outside my hut. Deeply buried beneath my consciousness there stirred the vague memory of a letter that I had written to Roland in those legendary days when I was still at Oxford, and could spend my Sundays in thinking of him while the organ echoed grandly through New College chapel . . . but on Armistice Day not even a lonely survivor drowning in black waves of memory could be left alone with her thoughts. A moment after the guns had subsided into sudden, palpitating silence, the other VAD from my ward dashed excitedly into the annex.

'Brittain! Brittain! did you hear the maroons? It's over – it's all over! Do let's come out and see what's happening!'

Mechanically I followed her into the road. As I stood there, stupidly rigid, long after the triumphant explosions from Westminster had turned into a distant crescendo of shouting, I saw a taxi-cab turn swiftly in from the Embankment towards the hospital. The next moment there was a cry for doctors and nurses from passers-by, for in rounding the corner, the taxi had knocked down a small elderly woman who in listening, like myself, to the wild noise of a world released from nightmare, had failed to observe its approach. As I hurried to her side I realized that she was all but dead and already passed speech. She seemed to have shrunk to the dimensions of a child with the sharp features of age, but on a tiny chalk-white face an expression of shocked surprise still. Had she been thinking, I wondered, when the taxi struck her, of her sons at the front, now safe? . . .

I made a circular tour to Kensington by way of the intoxicated West End. With aching persistence my thoughts went back to the dead and the strange irony of their fates – to Roland, gifted, ardent, ambitious, who had died without glory in the conscientious perform-ance of a routine job; to Victor and Geoffrey, gentle and different, who, conquering nature by resolution, had each gone down bravely in a big 'show'; and finally to Edward, musical, serene, a lover of peace, who had fought courageously through so many battles and at last had been killed while leading a vital counter-attack in one of the few decisive actions of the war. As I struggled through the waving, shrieking crowds in Piccadilly and Regent Street on the overloaded top of a 'bus', some witty enthusiast for contemporary history symbolically turned upside-down the sign-board 'Seven Kings'.

Late that evening, when supper was over, a group of elated VADS who were anxious to walk through Westminster and Whitehall to Buckingham Palace prevailed upon me to join them. Outside the Admiralty a crazy group of convalescent Tommies were collecting specimens of different uniforms and bundling their wearers into flag-strewn taxis; with a shout they seized two of my companions and disappeared into the clamorous crowds, waving flags and shaking rattles. Wherever we went, a burst of enthusiastic cheering greeted our Red Cross uniform and complete strangers adorned with wound stripes rushed up and shook me warmly by the hand.

. . . All those with whom I had really been intimate were gone; no one remained to share with me the heights and the depths of my memories. As the years went by and youth departed and remembrance grew dim, a deeper and ever deeper darkness would cover the young men who were once my contemporaries.

For the first time I realized, with all that full realization meant, how completely everything that had hitherto made up my life had vanished with Edward and Roland, with Victor and Geoffrey. The war was over; a new age was beginning; but the dead were dead and would never return.[85]

The nation had lost well over 600,000 of its younger men (leaving aside the substantial proportion of the 1.6 million who were gravely mutilated) amounting to about 9 per cent of all men under 55. In 1911, there had been 155 males aged between twenty and forty per thousand of the population in England and Wales; in 1921 for every thousand of the population, there were only 141. The balance of females over the age of fourteen, therefore, rose from 595 per thousand in 1911, to 638 per thousand in 1921, and the proportion of widows per thousand of the population rose from 38 to 43. In memoirs such as Vera Brittain's we glimpse something of the personal agony behind these cold statistics. For the working-class widow economic privation could make still worse the agony of personal loss.

Yet in revealing in her memoirs the shattering of a private life, Vera Brittain also, perhaps unwittingly, brings out how the narrow conventions of provincial middle-class life by which girls like her were confined in pre-war days were also shattered. Assessing the consequences of the war for British women involves working out a very complicated sum, which must include the tragedy and the suffering, and which must balance short-term gains and losses against long-term ones.

The political and legal story is relatively straightforward. After the General Election of December 1918, which returned the Conservative-dominated coalition Government under Lloyd George, the Government brought in a Sex Disqualification Act which opened jury service, the magistracy and the legal profession to women, and gave them qualified entry to the upper-reaches of the Civil Service; it was also made clear that there was in law no barrier to their full membership of the ancient universities of Oxford and Cambridge. At the end of 1919, with the establishment of a State Register of Nurses, nursing was for the first time recognized as a full profession. The National Insurance Acts of 1918, 1920, 1921 made women, as wage-earners, eligible for national insurance benefits. In 1928 political emancipation was completed when all women over 21 without qualification were given the vote.

Expansion of job opportunity was the central phenomenon of women's war experience (see Tables 1–4). Yet at first sight, it seems to have been a very short-lived one. In 1914, there were rather less than six million women in paid employment in Great Britain and Ireland. At the end of the war this had risen by well over $1\frac{1}{4}$ million to between $7\frac{1}{4}$ and $7\frac{1}{2}$ million. By 1920 almost two thirds of those who had entered employment during the war had left it again. A year later, with the onset of the long period of trade depression and unemployment, the figure for women's employment was not much higher than it had been in 1914. The slump, in fact, cut across the development of the war, driving many women back into domestic

service for example. In 1921 there were 213 women police: but these were
fixed in the economy cuts of 1922. But significant, if small, increases
remained in commercial and professional jobs. In the 1930s there was
again a steady expansion in the number of women in paid employment.
It has to be remembered that the understanding upon which most women
took employment during the war was that of a temporary contribution to
the National effort. There was an obligation to find jobs for soldiers
returning from the trenches. Prejudices, of course, remained; but then,
it was clearly the ambition of the vast majority of women to be wife and
mother. The terrible tragedy of the war was that for so many of them this
was denied.

In various ways the war marked a loosening of the standards of conventional morality. In February 1918 the National Council for the
Unmarried Mother and her child were founded. After the war, Marie
Stopes and her disciples set up the first birth control clinic. It seems
likely that the new freedoms ran more deeply than the surface evidence
would suggest. In public the British remained a prudish lot. Marie
Stopes's open advocacy of contraception was too much for traditional
opinion, and her greatest work, published just as the war came to an end,
had the highly moral title of *Married Love*. The attempt to popularize
her ideas through a film entitled *Maisy's Marriage* brings out the limits
of what was permissible in public performance. Birth control is allegedly
explained to Maisy through a sequence in which all we see is a garden
over-filled with roses, in which the unwanted blooms are pruned with a
pair of secateurs. Well might girls remain in confusion and ignorance if
this was all they had to go on. But, of course, word-of-mouth can be a
more potent medium of mass communication than any film.

The world, and women, had changed. Undoubtedly the changes for
women remained within the framework of a 'traditional' conception of
women's role in society. Yet within that framework – the terrible losses
of the war apart – the possibilities of a happier and more fulfilled life
were much greater. The marriage rate took an upward leap in 1915, which
has been sustained ever since; there was new provision for child nurture
and child care. Some of the sillier prejudices about women and society
had gone for good: feminists no longer had to argue as suffragettes had
done in warlike Edwardian times, that the women who died in childbirth
during the Boer War had 'lost their lives in service to the state'.[86] For
determined women, there were totally new professional opportunities.
The war, so horrible in so many ways, provided a unique and concentrated
experience. In the language of today, it provided a 'raising of consciousness'. The women who went back to domestic service insisted, as the
abundant evidence shows,[87] on less degrading conditions; many no
longer lived in. The same was true among shop assistants – where,
anyway, 'living in' had disappeared amid the food shortages of war. Many
of the effects were concealed by the onset of depression. Change is not
constant and not always in the one direction. There were many setbacks,
but many of the developments of more recent times had their distant
origins in the upheavals of the First World War.

OVERLEAF Armistice Day
group in US military vehicle,
11 November 1918

Table 1
Some Broad Census Data England and Wales Only

	Total Population	Total females	Over 10 years	Total females occupied	married	widowed	Females per 1,000 males	Females per 1,000 males in age group 20-4.
1901	32,527,843	16,799,230	13,189,585	4,171,751	917,509		1,068	
1911	36,070,492	18,624,884	14,357,113	4,830,734	680,191	411,011	1,068	1,09
			Over 12 years					
1921	37,886,699	19,811,460	15,699,805	5,065,332	693,034	425,981	1,096	1,17
			Over 14 years					
1931	39,952,377	20,819,367	16,419,894	5,606,043	896,702	389,187	1,088	

Table 2
Women in Munitions (Metal and Chemical Trades) – Great Britain and Ireland
Private Factories and Government Factories

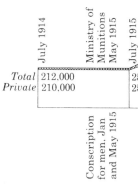

☐ *Private*   ▨ *Government*

	July 1914	Ministry of Munitions May 1915	July 1915	July 1916	July 1917	November 1918	
Total	212,000		256,000			819,000 / 616,000	947,000 / 700,000 ... 379, / 373,
Private	210,000		253,000				

Conscription for men, Jan and May 1915

Table 3 **Other Occupations** Great Britain and Ireland	1914	191
Transport	18,200	117,20
Municipal Tramways	1,200	18,80
Private	200	5,80
Buses	300	4,30
Railways	12,000	65,00
Commerce	505,200	934,50
Banking	1,500	37,60
Insurance	7,000	32,30
Agriculture	190,000	228,00
National and Local Government (including education)	262,200	460,20
Hotels, Public Houses, Theatres etc.	181,000	220,00
Industry	2,178,600	2,970,60
Textile trades	863,000	818,00
Clothing trades	612,000	556,00
Domestic Service	1,658,000	1,250,00
On own account or as Employers	430,000	470,00
Professional, home workers etc (including nurses, secretaries and typists)	542,000	652,50
Altogether in occupations	5,966,000	7,311,00
Not in occupations but over 10	12,946,000	12,496,00
Under 10	4,809,000	4,731,00
Total females	23,721,000	24,538,00

Table 4
Women in Professional Occupations England and Wales

	1911	1914	1918	1921	1931
Nurses	77,060	33,000	70,000	94,381	118,909
Doctors and Surgeons	477			1,253	2,810
Dentists	250			296	394
Civil Engineers	0			41	135
Architects	7			49	107
Chartered Accountants	19			43	119
Barristers (and in 1931, Judges and Stipendiary Magistrates)	0	0		20	79
(Law clerks c2,200 1911)					
Solicitors	0			17	116
Social Welfare workers	0			1,663	3,389
School Mistresses, Teachers, Professors, Lecturers	183,298			203,802	199,560

Table 5
Social Background of Women's Police Service

Total number trained and equipped   1,080

Certified women   167

Nurses   130

Teachers   75

Clerical   34

Business   59

Munitions workers   28

Shop assistants   13

Dressmakers, etc.   28

Land workers   9

Motor drivers   10

Doctors and chemists' assistants   6

Domestic   110

Women of private means or of no profession   411

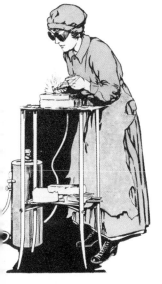

Table 6
The Nursing Services 1914–1918

	Queen Alexandra's Imperial Military Nursing Service, including the Reserve		Territorial Force Nursing Services	
	Trained	Untrained and partially trained	Trained	Untrained and partially trained
Aug 1914	463		2,783	
Aug 1915	4,126	389	4,129	1,268
Aug 1916	6,864	3,580	4,491	2,785
Aug 1917	6,711	4,074	4,525	4,179
Aug 1918	7,835	4,958	4,886	5,350
Nov 1918	7,710	5,407	5,059	5,490

Table 7
Growth of The VADs

	Men	Women
1st August 1914	23,047	47,196
1st April 1920	39,909	82,857

Table 8
Number of Women Employed with the British Expeditionary Force, France. August 1918.

Nursing sisters and others working for the Royal Army Medical Corps.

	Nurses	VADS	General Service VADS	Others	Total
British	2,396	1,685	862		4,94
Colonial	1,298	34		6	1,38
American	807	14		21	84
Totals	4,501	1,733	862	27	7,12

Nursing sisters and other workers in the British Red Cross Society

	Nurses	VADS	Others	Total
British Red Cross Society	216	592	54	86
St John Ambulance Brigade Hospital	55	26		8
Friends' Ambulance Unit	14	21		3
First Aid Nursing Yeomanry Corps		18	98	11
Totals	285	657	152	1,09

Queen Mary's Army Auxiliary Corps	7,808

Societies which employ women

YMCA	571
Church Army	77
Soldiers' Christian Association	54
Salvation Army	150
Other institutions	204
Totals	1,056

Other Government Departments which employ women as drivers

General Service VADS	99

Table 9
QMAAC: Strength by Months

Date	Officers	Other ranks Abroad	At Home	Total
1917				
August				2,377
September		2,280	815	3,095
October		2,900	2,340	5,240
November	462	3,496	12,310	16,228
December	397	4,105	15,696	20,198
1918				
January	456	4,779	17,244	22,479
February				
March	637	5,875	26,514	33,026
April	637	6,378	28,538	35,553
May	682	7,249	25,540	33,471
June	925	7,629	26,676	35,230
July	984	7,677	27,599	36,260
August	1,004	7,846	28,297	37,147
September	1,004	8,129	29,330	38,463
October	1,118	8,274	30,340	39,732
November	1,077	8,548	31,850	40,850
December	1,058	8,529	30,155	39,742
1919				
January	1,081	8,037	28,875	37,993
February	1,059	8,016	26,557	35,632
March	961	8,019	23,228	32,208
April	935	7,657	21,148	29,740
May	850	7,280	18,999	27,129
June	782	6,979	17,278	25,039
July	740	6,850	16,337	23,927
August	721	6,155	13,141	20,017
September	684	5,996	12,471	19,151
October	643	4,676	9,163	14,482
November	518	2,471	4,720	7,709
December	208	1,876	1,451	3,535
1920				
January	67	281	231	579
February	29	63	257	349
March	28	63	232	323
April*	28	61	195	284

* On 1st May, 1920, the Queen Mary's Army Auxiliary Corps ceased to exist.
Two officials & 63 other ranks were to be retained with D.G.R. and E. at St Pol
until 31st July, 1920.

References

The following abbreviations are used:

Wom. Coll. The Women's Collection in the Imperial War Museum
IWM   Other Collections in the Imperial War Museum
FL   Fawcett Library, London
LM   Museum of London
MPL   Manchester Public Library, Department of Archives
PRO   Public Record Office
NLS   Department of Manuscripts, National Library of Scotland

*Full information on the published works cited can be found in the
'Notes on Further Reading'.*

1   War Cabinet Committee on Women in Industry: Miss Smith's evidence,
    Monday 14 October 1918 (typed up from shorthand record). Wom. Coll, Emp. 70
2   NUWSS Circular, August 1914. MPL
3   LM (Item Z6467)
4   Grace Roe to Mrs Archdale, 21 November 1914. LM (Item Z6081)
5   Christabel Pankhurst,
    The War: A Speech Delivered At The London Opera House
    8 September 1914. LM
6   *Western Daily Mercury*, 17 November 1914
7   Central Committee on Women's Employment, leaflets, Wom. Coll. Emp. 3
8   M. Bondfield to M. Macarthur, 13 January 1915. Wom. Coll. Emp. 3
9   Letter from Mrs E. M. Garstang to IWM 27 October 1975
10 National Council of Women, *NCW Women Patrols 1914 to 1920* Wom. Coll.
    Emp. 42.7
11 LM (50,82/344)
12 NUWSS Council resolution, printed in NUWSS Circular, 9 March 1915. MPL
13 Mrs J. C. Teare to IWM December 1975
14 *Suffragette*, 16 April 1915
15 Wom. Coll. Emp. 48.2 and 48.3
16 Ministry of Munitions: Summary memorandum, June 1918. PRO. MUN. 5/349
17 Typescript survey by Miss C. V. Butler of the historical records branch.
    PRO. MUN. 5/349
18 Typescript account by Miss Dorothy T. Poole 1919. Wom. Coll. Mun. 17
19 Letter from Miss C. MacIver to IWM, 26 October 1975
20 Mrs H. A. Felstead to IWM, 27 January 1976
21 Memorandum by J. C. Burnham, Superintendent, and Ernest Taylor, Social
    Manager, HM Factory, Gretna, August 1919. Wom. Coll. Mun. 14
22 Memo by Ernest Taylor. Wom. Coll. Mun. 14
23 Manchester, Salford and District, Women's War Interests Committee, *Women
    in the Labour Market During the War* (n.d. 1916?) MPL
24 Agricultural Organizing Officer, Worcester to Board of Agriculture,
    14 September 1916. PRO. MAF 59/1
25 Letter from Mrs H. Parker to IWM, 5 November 1975
26 Letter from Mrs I. T. Middleton to IWM, 2 November 1975
27 Letter from Miss J. Tewkesbury to IWM, 21 October 1975
28 Typescript report 'Women Workers on the Land' (? June 1916). PRO. MAF 59/1
29 Wom. Coll. Land 5.1
30 Miss B. Goldingham to Mrs K. W. Furse, 23 February 1916. Wom. Coll. Emp. 43
31 Wom. Coll. Emp. 42.7
32 Wom. Coll. Emp. 42.2
33 Wom. Coll. Emp. 42.7
34 Mrs Furse's 'Draft letter to VAD Officers and Members' (n.d. Summer 1916 ?).
    Wom. Coll. BRC 10.1

35   Wom. Coll. BRC 10.1
36   Wom. Coll. B.R.C 10.3
37   Conference on the Organization of Women Employed by the Army, 5 January 1917. Wom. Coll. Army 3.9
38   Lord Derby's reply to minute from Adjutant-General, 25 January 1917. Wom. Coll. Army 3.6
39   Wom. Coll. Army 3.11
40   Wom. Coll. Army 3.7, 3.8, 3.9 and 3.12
41   Haig to War Office, 11 March 1917 (copy). Wom. Coll. Army 3.4
42   WAAC Headquarter's circular 37. Wom. Coll. Army 3.13
43   Minutes of 41st Meeting of Central Joint VAD Committee, 1 November 1917. Wom. Coll. BRC 10.8
44   K. Furse to Maud Royden, 6 November 1917 (copy). Wom. Coll. BRC 10.8
45   Interview with Mrs Chalmers Watson, 19 June 1918. Wom. Coll. Army 3.12
46   Letter from Mrs Elsie Cooper to IWM, 23 January 1976
47   Letter from Miss Violet E. Le Fleming Frend to IWM, 30 December 1975
48   Copy of letter to Mrs Furse in Wom. Coll. BRC 10.3
49   Wom. Coll. Army 3.14. WAAC circular 30, 22 January 1918
50   PRO MAF 42/8
51   Note by Mairi Chisholm of Chisholm, 1975
52   Wom. Coll. DEC 5
53   Wom. Coll. BRC 25.8
54   Wom. Coll. Emp. 42.2
55   'Report on Industrial Welfare conditions in Coventry' November 1916. Wom. Coll. Emp. 45.7
56   Note by secretary of the War Babies and Mothers' League, 1915. Wom. Coll. BO4
57   R. Strachey (Ed.), *Our Freedom*, p.251
58   *The War In Its Effect on Women*, August 1916
59   British Dominions Woman Suffrage Union, *Report of the second (Biennial) conference*, London 1916. Wom. Coll. Suf. 11
60   Miss Patricia Vernon to IWM, 1975
61   WAAC Circular. DCC 64, 8 April 1918. Wom. Coll. Army 3.14
62   Ministry of Labour M. 40/56, 1918. Wom. Coll. Army 3.28
63   Nurse Rendel to her mother, 21 September 1918. IWM, FER 3
64   *Observer*, 8 April 1917
65   W. Robertson (Ed.), *Middlesborough's Effort In The Great War*, n.d., pp. 169–70, 184–5
66   Wom. Coll. B.O.5.4
67   Board of Education, *Correspondence Relating to School Attendance 1915*
68   M. Cosens, *Lloyd George's Munitions Girls*, 1916
69   Wom. Coll. BRC 24.1
70   'Women's work in the postal censorship'. Wom. Coll. Emp. 52
71   'Report on VAD work', 13 July 1916. Wom. Coll. BRC 10.2
72   WAAC circular 9, 30 October 1917. Wom. Coll. Army 3.14
73   PRO. Reco. 1/747
74   Minutes of Women's Interests Committee, 8 February and report of Women's Interests Committee, April 1916. Wom. Coll. Sof. 1. *Common Cause*, 16 June 1916
75   War Cabinet Committee Meeting on Women in Industry, minutes of evidence, 14 October 1918 (Typescript) Wom. Coll. Emp. 70
76   War Cabinet Committee on Women in Industry (Physiological Sub-Committee), minutes of evidence November 1918. Wom. Coll. Emp. 70
77   Ibid.
78   *Report of the Committee on Women in Industry: appendices, summaries of evidence.* (Cmd. 167, 1919) p. 204
79   FL 367. Also Sylvia Pankhurst papers, file 27
80   *Common Cause*, 19 May 1916
81   PRO CAB Doc. XIV(2), 9 March 1916, and 12 July 1916, cited by Morgan, p. 138
82   Pugh, p. 363
83   FL 340. But see Sylvia Pankhurst papers, file 21
84   Pugh, p. 370
85   *Testament of Youth*, pp 460–63
86   Miss Jamie Allan's Suffragette Papers, NLS Acc. 4498
87   Some of it cited by Ruth Adam, pp. 74–5

Notes on further reading

The recent historical works mentioned in the Preface are as follows:

Arthur Marwick — *The Deluge: British Society and the First World War* (first published in 1965, republished 1968 and 1973);

Ruth Adam — *A Woman's Place* (1975)

Roger Fulford — *Votes for Women* (1957)

Constance Rover — *Woman's Suffrage and Party Politics* (1967)

Antonia Raeburn — *The Militant Suffragettes* (1973)

Andrew Rosen — *Rise up Women!* (1974)

Martin D. Pugh — 'Politicians and the Woman's Vote 1914–1918' in *History* volume 59, No. 197, October 1974

David Morgan — *Suffragists and Liberals* (1975)

David Mitchell — *Women on the Warpath* (1966)

David Mitchell — *The Fighting Pankhursts* (1967)

Midge McKenzie — *Shoulder to Shoulder* (1975) is a well illustrated scrap-book containing some important documents

Elizabeth Ewing — *Women in Uniform through the Centuries* (1975) is useful.

J. M. Winter — 'Some Aspects of the Demographic Consequences of the First World War in Britain', *Population Studies*, November 1975. See also his 'Some Aspects of the impact of the First World War on Civilian Health', *Economic History Review*, December 1976

Autobiographies and memoirs of special interest are:

Vera Brittain — *Testament of Youth* (1936)

Irene Clephane — *Towards Sex Freedom* (1936)

Margaret Cole — *Growing up into Revolution* (1949)

Millicent Garrett Fawcett — *The Women's Victory and After: Personal Reminiscenses 1911–1918* (1920)

Annie Kenney — *Memoirs of a Militant* (1924)

Marchioness of Londonderry — *Retrospect* (1938)

Christabel Pankhurst — *Unshackled* (1959)

Sylvia Pankhurst — *The Home Front* (1932)

Mrs C. S. Peel — *How We Lived Then 1914–1918* (1929)

Ray Strachey (Ed.) — *Our Victory and After* (1936)

M. Cole (Ed.) — *Beatrice Webb's Diaries, 1912–1934* (1952)

I have discussed the main archive sources in the Preface. The most important Government Papers which contain much factual information as well as being illuminating on official attitudes are:

Board of Trade *Report on Increased Employment of Women*, Cd.9164, of 1918;
Report of the Committee on Women's Employment, Cd.9239 of 1918 and
Report of the War Cabinet Committee on Women in Industry, Cmd. 135 of 1919

Index

(Page numbers in italics refer to illustrations)